Praise f

Studying to preach can be the best of times and the worst of times. There are days when it all flows so quickly you can hardly write fast enough to keep up. The passage falls into a perfect outline as soon as you open your Bible. Other times it feels like trying to wrestle an octopus into a straightjacket . . . in the dark! Whether you're a seasoned preacher or you are just cutting your milk teeth, this book will help you.

LEVI LUSKO

Pastor of Fresh Life Church in Montana

Author of *Swipe Right: The Life-and-Death Power of Sex and Romance*

Time management is a continual struggle of pastoral ministry. Sermon preparation usually suffers the collateral damage. In *8 Hours or Less*, Ryan Huguley will show you how to faithfully preach the Word and steward your time. Read this book for wise, practical advice for your weekly ministry of the Word.

H. B. CHARLES JR.

Pastor, Shiloh Metropolitan Baptist Church in Jacksonville, FL

Author of *It Happens After Prayer: Biblical Motivation for Believing Prayer*

I most often recommend the classic works on preaching to those I coach and mentor, and I will now be adding Pastor Ryan's book, *8 Hours or Less*. Ryan has planted a church and now pastors a large congregation, so he understands the demands of pastoral ministry and the need to maximize preparation time in the development of a sermon. This is an insightful and practical book that will help both the experienced expositor of Scripture as well as those stepping up to the pulpit for the first time.

JOE THORN

Pastor of Redeemer Fellowship in St. Charles, IL

Author of *The Heart of the Church, The Character of the Church,* and *The Life of the Church*

With all the demands of pastoral ministry, it is easy to allow our sermon preparation to slide. In this powerful and practical book, Ryan shows us how to make the most of our time and still preach biblical and helpful sermons. I wish I had read this book years ago. I highly recommend it!

GREG SURRATT

Founding pastor of Seacoast Church in South Carolina
President of the Association of Related Churches (ARC)

As a preaching pastor, I'm well aware of how time can slip away in the study with lexicons, commentaries, maps, background research, and the hermeneutical challenges that accompany weekly sermon prep. Ryan's done a good job of explaining the craft of building a strong sermon in a reasonable amount of time. This will help pastors make the most of their time in the study so they can have ample time for their church, family, and the rest of life.

ALEX EARLY

Preaching and Theology Pastor, Redemption Church in Seattle, WA
Author of *The New Believer's Guide to the Christian Life*

I am continually amazed at how busy my life gets as a pastor. Staff meetings, counseling, and leadership development take up a ton of time, as they should. But perhaps the most important thing I do each week is to prepare a sermon to feed God's people. This book is a great tool for every pastor who wants to maximize his time for God's glory in preaching the gospel for the good of the church.

BRYAN MOWREY

Pastor, Jubilee Church in Saint Louis, MO
Movement leader, New Frontiers USA

FOREWORD BY JAMES MACDONALD

8 HOURS OR LESS

WRITING FAITHFUL SERMONS FASTER

RYAN HUGULEY

MOODY PUBLISHERS

CHICAGO

Scripture quotations are from the ESV® Bible (The Holy Bible, English Standard Version®), copyright © 2001 by Crossway, a publishing ministry of Good News Publishers. Used by permission. All rights reserved.

Edited by Kevin P. Emmert
Interior Design: Ragont Design
Cover Design: Erik M. Peterson
Cover illustration of clock face copyright © 2017 by Prixel Creative/ Lightstock (331295). All rights reserved.

All websites and phone numbers listed herein are accurate at the time of publication but may change in the future or cease to exist. The listing of website references and resources does not imply publisher endorsement of the site's entire contents. Groups and organizations are listed for informational purposes, and listing does not imply publisher endorsement of their activities.

Library of Congress Cataloging-in-Publication Data

Names: Huguley, Ryan, author.
Title: 8 hours, or less : writing faithful sermons faster / Ryan Huguley.
Other titles: Eight hours, or less
Description: Chicago : Moody Publishers, 2017. | Includes bibliographical references.
Identifiers: LCCN 2017000712 (print) | LCCN 2017011695 (ebook) | ISBN 9780802495198 () | ISBN 9780802415080
Subjects: LCSH: Preaching.
Classification: LCC BV4211.3 (ebook) | LCC BV4211.3 .H844 2017 (print) | DDC
  251/.01--dc23
LC record available at https://lccn.loc.gov/2017000712

We hope you enjoy this book from Moody Publishers. Our goal is to provide high-quality, thought-provoking books and products that connect truth to your real needs and challenges. For more information on other books and products written and produced from a biblical perspective, go to www.moodypublishers.com or write to:

Moody Publishers
820 N. LaSalle Boulevard
Chicago, IL 60610

1 3 5 7 9 10 8 6 4 2

Printed in the United States of America

To Redemption Bible Church
for listening graciously to me as I learned to preach

CONTENTS

FOREWORD

There is nothing I love more than preaching, and there is no preacher I have greater affection for than Ryan Huguley. Like all of us, he is a man *in process*. God is working a wonderful sanctification in Ryan—and it flows into and through his preaching with a life-giving authenticity that greatly impacts his hearers.

However, Ryan is not just a man *in process*, he is also a man *of process*. While some shine in the pastoral or administrative functions of the ministry, Ryan excels at process. He is keenly aware of time-wasters, energy-depleters, and many ways to get more out of the hours you expend in building Christ's kingdom.

In *8 Hours or Less*, Ryan brings his process strength to bear upon the task of preaching and shows us how to get much more from every hour, day, and week of sermon prep.

Read his ideas, and try his proven methods. You will have a better week, and your church family will hear much better messages.

DR. JAMES MACDONALD
Founding and Senior Pastor of Harvest Bible Chapel

INTRODUCTION

"I love to preach. I hate preparing to preach."

I must have said this to countless people over the past seven years. Preaching is by far my favorite part of pastoring, but the stress, sweat, and tears that preparing to preach requires has caused to me to wake up on more than one Monday longing for the days when my only job was slinging espresso at Starbucks.

Every week went like this: Sunday morning I would finish preaching my sermon, pray with a few people, meet some guests, and help pack up equipment, since we were a mobile church. I would then climb into my truck to head home, high on all God had just accomplished in our time together as His church. For those brief hours, all the work of preparation was eclipsed by the fruit I was privileged to watch the Spirit of God produce through it. But before I even made it to the first stoplight, this momentary high was chased off by the realization that tomorrow I had to start the entire process over again. Monday meant another text of Scripture, another blank page, and yet another sermon to prepare. With every day that passed, the pressure increased. The clock was ticking. Sunday was coming. I spent all day Friday staring at the cursor, trying to wrestle every word out of my heart and onto the page.

Every Saturday night I had recurring dreams of stepping up to preach but having nothing prepared—an obvious outworking of my insecurity.

I spent almost six years living like that. Prior to planting our church, I had been a worship pastor with limited preaching experience. I'd never had the privilege of taking a preaching class. (Although, I have come to learn that many who have still do not know how to effectively prepare a sermon.) I listened to various preachers incessantly and read every book on preaching that I could get my hands on. Yet no matter how much I listened and how much I read, sermon preparation continued stealing precious time. Responsible for counseling members, coaching budding leaders, and caring for our young church, I could not afford to continue spending fifteen to twenty hours a week trying to write a fresh sermon. In addition to stealing my time, preparation also began to steal my sanity. I had moments when I was unsure the joy of preaching for 40 minutes on Sunday was worth the 10,040 minutes of stress throughout the rest of the week.

If you are a preacher, my guess is that you can empathize with at least some of my pain, as differing versions of it are shared by us all. You may not want to say it out loud, and you may not even want to admit it to yourself, but you've probably wondered whether it all is truly worthwhile. And you've probably questioned, *Is it this difficult for every preacher every week?*

These sorts of questions finally caused me to take a more sobering look at my preparation process. What I found was that I did not really have one. Sure, I knew how to exegete a text. I knew how to write a detailed outline. Gutting out a manuscript each week had even helped me learn how to write . . .

a bit. What I did *not* have was a consistent and efficient step-by-step process to make preparation more sustainable. So that is what I set out to create. The result was a far less painful and far more enjoyable process broken up across my week, with clear daily milestones and firm time constraints that freed me to spend more time ruminating on my sermon and less time sitting at my desk staring at the computer.

Believe it or not, the time I now spend preparing at my desk in a given week averages eight hours or less.

You may read that and be tempted to throw away this book, convinced that I am a charlatan selling sermon-prep snake oil. But stick with me. I am not saying it takes only eight hours to prepare a sermon. I am a firm believer that the preacher is never finished prepping his sermon until after he has preached it. What I am saying is that more time sitting at your desk does not always guarantee a better product in the pulpit. I am also saying that if you are spending fifteen, twenty, or thirty hours a week preparing your sermon, you are probably doing it wrong. There is a way to prepare faithful sermons faster, and my hope is to humbly help you cut down on your own prep while also writing better sermons.

I have discovered three essential keys to spending eight hours or less at the desk.

DIVIDED WORK

In high school, I developed the bad habit of saving my writing for the last minute. My parents told me repeatedly that I should work ahead and write a little each day, but I ignored them and usually waited until a few hours before an assignment was due. This was a stressful way for me to work. As a result, I dreaded writing, which seemed to me a tortuous task. Sadly, I brought the same bad habits in my sermon preparation.

I used to do limited preparation on Monday—typically textual work—and the bulk of my writing on Friday. This made Friday the longest and worst day of my week. While everyone else woke up thinking, *TGIF!* (thank God it's Friday), I woke up thinking, *DGIF!* (dear God, it's Friday).

Dividing my work across the entirety of my week has sped up my process exponentially. I do textual work and outlining on Monday and group preparation on Tuesday. I write my introduction on Wednesday and my closing on Thursday. On Friday I fill in the outline. This alleviates the pressure that one day of prep puts on the preacher. If all you do is divide your work across the week, you will notice a massive difference. But I also encourage you to set daily milestones.

DAILY MILESTONES

My wife, Tami, and I went to Oahu, Hawaii, to celebrate our tenth wedding anniversary. One highlight of our trip was taking an unbelievable hike up to the Ka'au Crater on the east side of the island. I made some serious mistakes in preparing for the hike. For instance, I didn't actually prepare for the hike. I had read online that the hike would be an incredible experience. But if I had kept reading, I would have learned that it would also be insanely difficult. The hike is stretched along four beautiful yet treacherous miles, requiring you to inch along rainforest cliffs, climb beside waterfalls, and attentively keep track of the ever-changing trail. Truthfully, keeping track of the trail was the hardest part because it was marked only by the occasional tiny pink ribbon. On more than one occasion, a slight panic set in as we realized we had not seen any ribbons in a while, causing us to wonder, *Are we literally lost on the very island where they filmed the show* Lost? Inevitably, however, we would see a ribbon and be reminded that we were still on the trail.

Sometimes sermon prep feels like that. We know Sunday is coming and hope that we have what we need, that we are on the right track, and that we will have a whole sermon come Sunday. Setting clear daily milestones for my preparation has alleviated the wondering and worrying. I not only work a little bit each day, but also have specific goals for each day that keep me on track.

The last practice that has sped up my preparation significantly is setting determined deadlines for myself.

DETERMINED DEADLINES

Deadlines have a way of refining our focus and driving us to get things done. I have seen this in my physical health and fitness over the last few years. A decade of eating garbage and treating exercise like the plague left me overweight and out of shape. It's not that I didn't try to correct my bad habits. I had developed plans and made commitments, but I couldn't gain momentum. Nothing seemed to stick. Like most people, I was looking for "the secret." I have since learned there is no secret outside of discipline and hard work. But one decision did prove to be a turning point for me: I signed up for a Spartan Race. Perhaps you have heard about them. They are adventure races filled with tortuous terrain and obstacles like rope climbs, spear throws, and fire pits—yes, fire. I was intimidated when I signed up, but the fear really settled in when I had to sign a waiver acknowleding I was aware I might die! The deadline of that race lit a fear-fueled fire in me that forced me to get serious about my health and fitness. To date, I have lost over twenty pounds and am in the best shape of my life. But it would not have happened without a deadline. Where there is no deadline, there is no drive.

I believe this is why so many preachers do the bulk of their sermon prep on Fridays and Saturdays. The Sunday deadline drives us to focus and finish. Yet we need daily deadlines, not just weekly ones. Setting determined deadlines on my daily calendar has helped me greatly. Knowing I have an allotted time each day helps me finish my sermon by Saturday so that Sunday is not awkward for all.

The truth is that most of the pain in sermon preparation is the result of implementing a defective process. My goal is to help you evaluate, rethink, and refine your process. In chapter 1, we will define a "faithful" sermon so that we are on the same page regarding our goals. In chapters 2–6, we will establish daily milestones for each day of the week and look at some tools to help us stay within our desired time frame. Chapter 7 will explore how to maximize time on Sunday morning just prior to preaching. We will finish by discussing the importance of working the entire process.

Preaching will always result in pain. Preaching is war. Each week we work with the Holy Spirit to battle for the hearts, minds, and affections of those God has entrusted to us. No process will ever take away the pain of shepherding through preaching. Yet if we divide the work, establish daily milestones, and set determined deadlines, preparation need not suck us dry.

You *can* spend eight hours or less at the desk. If you are tired of being tired of sermon preparation, this book is for you. Turn the page, and together we will discover the joy of writing faithful sermons faster.

1

DEFINING A FAITHFUL SERMON

Would you embark on a vacation without first deciding where to go? I'm guessing no. If you don't know where you're headed, you won't know what to take with you or how to get there. What you'd pack for a February weekend in Chicago is far different than what you'd pack for a weekend in San Diego over the same time of year. You can't even punch an address into your GPS if you don't first determine your destination.

When my then girlfriend, now wife, Tami, attended college in downtown Chicago, I frequently visited her for the day and hung out by myself while she was in class. This was my first experience using the L-train system to get around. If you've never taken the L, trust me when I say that it's functional but no fun at all. It smells sort of like a urinal and feels like a cage. The problem for me was I never knew where I was or how to get anywhere. Every time Tami told me we had arrived at our stop, I would blast out of the doors in whatever direction I felt drawn toward, though I had no idea where we were going. Poor Tami was constantly calling me back from my determined drudge in the wrong direction. You have to know where you're headed if you're to have any hope of arriving there.

The same is true of a sermon. If we don't start with a strong understanding of what constitutes a faithful sermon, we won't even know where to begin. Remember, our goal is not simply to write sermons faster; it's to write *faithful* sermons faster. We're not just trying to find a quicker way to throw something together for Sunday. As shepherds of God's flock (1 Peter 5:2), we are called to feed His sheep (John 21:15–17). This means that every week we should feel the burden of serving a healthy, life-giving meal to God's people. So before we embark on our journey, we need to determine our destination. If we hope to arrive at a faithful sermon, we need to know just what that is.

WHAT A FAITHFUL SERMON IS NOT

First, let's start by clarifying what a faithful sermon is *not*.

A faithful sermon is not merely commentary. A good commentary sheds light on the original meaning of a text. As a preacher, I'm thankful for good commentaries. As you'll see in the next chapter, I believe commentaries are critical tools for any pastor. A carpenter needs a solid hammer. A photographer needs a professional-grade camera. And a pastor needs good commentaries. They are essential to the process of faithful exegesis—that is, drawing out the original meaning of the text. The problem is that a commentary is not a sermon. If all you do each Sunday is stand up and explain what the text says, you're not doing the full work of faithful preaching. A faithful sermon is never less than explaining the text, but it is certainly more.

A faithful sermon is not an inspirational talk. TED Talks have become hugely popular. If you're unfamiliar with this phenomenon, TED is "a nonprofit devoted to spreading ideas, usually in the form of short, powerful talks (18 minutes or less)."[1] Started in 1984 as a conference where technology, education, and design converged, TED now hosts conferences all over the world, and their talks have been watched millions of times online. I've seen a number of TED Talks myself and have to say that every single one, regardless of the subject matter, has compelled and inspired me.

Many preachers have observed the success of TED and have sought to shape their sermons along the same lines. This isn't all bad. We have much to learn from any effective communicator or communication style. The problem lies in the fact that preachers aren't meant to be mere inspirational speakers. That's not to say a sermon should never be inspirational; in fact, it should be. The difference is that we don't rely on our rhetorical abilities or intellects to inspire change in people's hearts. The Spirit of God uses the Word of God to change the people of God. Preachers don't rely on their own gifts or the power of their good ideas. Preachers rely on God.

A faithful sermon is not self-help instruction. Peruse any Barnes & Noble bookstore and you will find the self-help section to be one of the—if not *the*—largest in the store. We all have a deep-seated feeling that something about us is broken. Hence our insatiable appetite for books, blogs, and seminars that promise us change and healing. The problem is that we can't self-help what's truly broken in us. Sure, we can change some rudimentary behaviors, but we can't redeem what's gone wrong in our hearts. If what we needed was something we could do ourselves, then we would have no need for a Savior. This does not mean, however, that our sermons should not be helpful. The Bible is helpful. What we have to combat is the poisonous theology that says you and I, as well as those we have the privilege of preaching to each week, have the ability to transform ourselves. If your sermons "How to Have a Healthy Marriage" or "Five Ways to Better Manage God's Money" are not steeped in the reality that we are powerless apart from the redeeming work of Christ and the empowering work of His Spirit, people may leave encouraged, but they won't leave helped.

WHAT A FAITHFUL SERMON IS

Now, if a sermon is not a recapped commentary, an inspirational talk, or a self-help guide, what exactly constitutes a faithful sermon? While we could find many marks to categorize a faithful sermon, I'll keep my list to five.

Saturated in Scripture

Paul tells Timothy, the young pastor at Ephesus, to "preach the word" (2 Tim. 4:2). The same call hangs over every pulpit today. Sadly, when we survey some of what constitutes "preaching" today, we find what might seem like everything but the Word of God. Many sermons today are filled with more pop psychology and sociological analysis than Scripture. Too many sound more like political stump speeches than proclamations of God's authoritative Word. We must understand that there is absolutely no place in preaching for our own opinions, soapboxes, or political agendas. If you are a

Christian preacher, make no mistake: you are called to preach God's Word.

There has been and will continue to be much debate around how best to carry out this call. The reason for the debate is that there are a number of ways to preach God's Word. I have a personal aversion to the "my-way-is-the-only-way" attitude. Unless explicitly stated in God's Word, we have to hold our preferences with an open hand. This is especially true when it comes to any discussion surrounding how to best preach the Word. The most frequent debate seems to be over topical versus expository preaching.

Topical preaching seeks to relay what the Bible says about any particular topic. The sermon is based on a simple question: "What does the Bible say about _____?" When done well, the sermon surveys what Scripture says about the topic, doctrine, or issue at hand.

Topical preaching has its strengths. First, it helps people see the consistency of God's Word. Second, it helps people understand the full scope of what God says about particular issues. Third, it helps preachers address particular areas of confusion, disbelief, disobedience, or biblical deficiency that may exist among their people. Crafting shorter series and covering a wide variety of topics over the course of a year can be especially helpful if the population one pastors is more transient in nature.

But topical preaching also has at least three liabilities. First, you may overlook a critical verse while discussing a particular topic. The Bible is a big book! Every time I preach a topical sermon, I fear I may miss a verse that sheds light on my topic. If we say only part of what God says, we risk skewing all of what He says. Because the question topical preaching seeks to answer is, "What does the Bible say about _____?", a great amount of time, effort, and care must be given to ensuring you can truly answer the question. That's not to say it can't be done. It just means you run the risk of missing something while trying to answer the question.

Second, you may preach only your pet topics. If I plan my preaching calendar around topics, I will be more inclined to select ones I want to address and less inclined to take on the ones I don't want to address. Preachers are human. That means most of us don't like tackling topics with which we are unfamiliar or that are rife with conflict and controversy. With the exception of those who tend to be brash and combative, most preachers avoid potential land mines. The Bible is filled with countercultural and difficult truths, teaching that rubs against every part of our flesh as fallen people. In my experience, God seems to care little for what we deem politically correct. If topics alone drive our preaching decisions, we may find ourselves avoiding those things we simply don't want to deal with.

Third, you may fail to teach people how to read the Bible. The greatest weakness of topical preaching is that it doesn't always instruct listeners how to read and interpret the Bible. For a long time I sat under topical preaching almost exclusively, and I would find myself walking away impressed by the preacher's ability to find an array of relevant material in the Bible but insecure about my own ability to do so. It also didn't teach me about context—that every verse has additional pertinent verses that come before and after. It didn't force me to see that each verse is part of a larger book that is part of a Testament that is part of a metanarrative. If preachers aren't careful to teach the context of Scripture, listeners won't know who wrote each book and why. Ultimately, topical preaching doesn't effectively help people understand how the Bible is put together, how it should be read, and how it can be prayerfully studied.

If you are to faithfully shepherd a body of God's people, topical preaching will need to be a necessary weapon in your preaching arsenal. As a fellow pastor, however, I would encourage you not to make it the steady diet you feed God's people due to the liabilities mentioned above. Instead, use expository preaching as the main style and source of your weekly preaching ministry.

Differing definitions for what constitutes expository preaching abound. Bryan Chapell writes, "The technical definition of an expository sermon requires that it expound Scripture by deriving from a specific text main points and subpoints that disclose the thought of the author, cover the scope of the passage, and are applied to the lives of listeners."[2] More succinctly, Jason Meyer defines it as "stewarding and heralding God's word in such a way that people encounter God through his word."[3] One of my personal favorites is from Mark Dever, who says, "Expositional preaching is preaching in which the main point of the biblical text being considered becomes the main point of the sermon being preached."[4] In the simplest sense, expositional preaching takes one text and draws out the author's original intent. You start with a passage and build the sermon around it. It is the opposite of having something you want to say and then finding a text to support it. It is textually driven preaching.

Perhaps the greatest strength of expository preaching is

that is demonstrates to listeners how to read the Bible. Faithful exposition forces us to take into account the context of the passage. You have to know the author, the audience, the setting, and the purpose for which it was written. You have to understand how all the other material surrounding the text informs the way you read and understand it. These are skills all Christians should employ every time they read Scripture, not just when preachers preach. When I do this well as a preacher, my sermon not only faithfully relays God's Word to my people, but also demonstrates how listeners can read the Bible for themselves.

Expository preaching also forces you to discuss difficult topics. If topical preaching encourages you to preach your pet topics and to avoid difficult ones, expository preaching does the opposite. As preachers, we are often averse to preaching difficult, confusing, controversial, or awkward topics. If you choose to be an expository preacher, and especially if you preach verse by verse through entire books of the Bible, you won't have the luxury of skipping topics. If it's in the text, you'll have to deal with it.

My hope is that you choose to build the legacy of your preaching ministry on biblical exposition, with some topical preaching mixed in, to best serve your people. While you have some liberty in *how* you preach, you have none regarding *what* you preach. We are called to preach the Word. Regardless of whether you choose an expositional, topical, narrative, evangelistic, or any other style, make absolutely certain that your preaching is not sprinkled but rather saturated with and driven by the Word of God.

Christ Centered

The Bible is not a disconnected mix of moral fables that point you toward a happier life. The entire Bible, from beginning to end, is the true story of God reconciling the world to Himself through the person and work of Jesus Christ. That means the whole Bible is about Jesus.

In Luke 24, Jesus walks a couple of His disciples through the Bible study to end all Bible studies. Luke tells us, "And beginning with Moses and all the Prophets, he interpreted to them in all the Scriptures *the things concerning himself*" (v. 27, emphasis added). This means we can't preach Christ only from the New Testament, because Jesus was specifically walking them through the Old. The Old Testament anticipates the coming of Christ. The New Testament announces His arrival, declares His message, and then anticipates His return. So if Christ isn't in our sermons, we aren't preaching faithful ones. As the great British preacher Charles Spurgeon once said, "Let your sermons be full of Christ, from beginning to end crammed full of the gospel."[5] That's what we're after: sermons crammed full of Christ.

Culturally Contextualized

To contextualize something is simply to bring it into the present context—meaning the present language, setting, and situation. Contextualization has received a steady stream of criticism in recent years. What I find curious about such criticism is that we all contextualize. When you travel abroad and stumble through a sad but sincere attempt to order your latte in the native tongue, you're doing the work of contextualization. As a preacher, whether you wear jeans and a T-shirt or a three-piece suit while preaching, you're contextualizing. If you're not preaching the New Testament in Greek each Sunday, you're contextualizing.

I do, however, understand the concern and believe caution is necessary. The fear is that if we *contextualize* the message, we will somehow *compromise* it. This criticism assumes we may be attempting to soften biblical imperatives. If we're pulling proverbial punches for fear of offending modern ears, we're not contextualizing—we're stripping the message of its truth and power. When done correctly, though, contextualization does not compromise. In contextualizing, we simply labor to make the original meaning of the ancient text clearer to modern ears. Even Jesus contextualized when He drew images from first-century agrarian settings to teach His parables. When Jesus spoke of farmers (Matt. 13:3–9), shepherds (John 10), and vineyards (Matt. 20:1–16), he was contextualizing. He was using everyday references to convey eternal truths. That is our task as well. At no point are we to distort or dumb down the text, but we are to lead our listeners back into its historical setting and meaning by using language, imagery, and ideas that people can understand.

Directed to the Whole Person

God's Spirit is in the business of using His Word to completely transform His people (see Rom. 12:2). This means the job of the preacher is to bring the whole message of God's Word to bear on the whole person. Our minds, hearts, and behaviors should be progressively changed as we sit under the authority of God's Word. Unfortunately, much preaching defaults to reaching only the mind or heart or behavior—rather than informing all three.

We preach to the head. Romans 12:2 says, "Do not be conformed to this world, but be transformed by the renewal of your *mind*" (emphasis added). All change, transformation, and renewal starts in the mind, which means we better be preaching to the heads of those listening. A sermon is not a Hallmark movie. The goal is not just to make people cry, feel good, or walk away encouraged by mere sentiment. We can't restrict our preaching to emotions; we also have to preach to the mind. That means we have to anticipate objections, dismantle doubt, and respond to skepticism with reason. We have to deal with the text as a matter of fact and skillfully explain, illustrate, and apply it to the thought patterns of God's people.

We preach to the heart. While faithful preaching should first emphasize the renewal of the mind, it need not avoid passion and emotion. Many pastors, however, are leery of appealing to people's feelings. Their caution is understandable and, in many cases, wise.

We live in a feelings-driven culture. Everyone is encouraged to "follow your heart." That's great advice if you're a Disney princess, but it's devastating if you're an actual person living in the real world. Our feelings don't always indicate what is real. We are not to be led by our hearts; instead, our minds should drive the way we feel, and good pastors know this. They don't want to be guilty of manipulating people's emotions to get a momentary response, so they steer clear of this area altogether. But God has given us the capacity to experience things deeply and to respond intensely, and to neglect this aspect of the human experience is to neglect a critical part of those we're called to shepherd.

To preach to the heart means to preach to the center of who a person is—their motives, passions, and desires. Jesus was amazing at this. After His mind-blowing, life-changing conversation with two of the disciples on the Emmaus road just after His resurrection, they said, "Did not our hearts burn within us while he talked to us on the road, while he opened to us the Scriptures?" (Luke 24:32). Jesus changed their minds as He helped them rethink the meaning of the Old Testament, showing them that it was ultimately about Him (Luke 24:27). And this shift in their thinking made them feel differently. Their hearts burned inside them with the realization that this news changed everything. This is what we're after every week! We want people's hearts to burn within them. Our goal is to leave listeners feeling entirely different about whatever subject we're addressing because we've preached first to their minds and then to their hearts.

We preach to the hands. Preaching to the mind and heart should leave people thinking a simple question: *So, what should I do?* It's a question of application and implication. Other questions include: *What action are we supposed to take in light of what we've just heard? Why does this matter?* These are the right kind of questions to ask every time we come to God's Word.

In John 13:17, Jesus said, "If you know these things, blessed are you if you *do* them" (emphasis added). Knowledge without action is worthless. Unfortunately, I hear a fair amount of preaching that does little to help people sort out the implications of the information conveyed in Scripture. We've already established that faithful preaching is not a self-help seminar, but that it should be helpful. At the very least, we need to help people start thinking through the implications of every text in their daily lives. (We'll discuss this more in chapter 6.)

We need to have the humility and self-awareness to acknowledge that preaching to one of these three aspects of a person typically comes more naturally to us than preaching to all three. Your own wiring, theological presuppositions, and personal experiences tend to point you toward one direction more than the others. For instance, if you're academically minded, you may naturally preach more to the head. If you're more relationally minded, you may default to the heart. If you're more missionally minded or action oriented, you may emphasize the hands. The key is knowing yourself and intentionally preaching to the entire person—the head, heart, and hands.

Proclaimed Boldly

Faithful preaching is not just *what* you say, but also *how* you communicate it. As Paul concluded his letter to the Ephesians, he petitioned them to pray on his behalf. Notice his request:

> To that end keep alert with all perseverance, making supplication for all the saints, and also for me, that words may be given to me in opening my mouth *boldly* to proclaim the mystery of the gospel, for which I am an ambassador in chains, that I may declare it *boldly, as I ought to speak.* (6:18–20, emphasis added)

Of all that he could have asked prayer for, he mentioned boldness. According to Paul, faithful preaching should have a specific tone. Our sermons should be marked not by apology, equivocation, or timidity. Biblical preaching is marked by boldness. That boldness is given by the Spirit of God and bound up in our conviction that the Word of God is actually true and thus crucial for people to understand and obey. Most of us don't like starting conflict, making others feel uncomfortable, or ruffling people's feathers. But we have to love people more than we love their comfort and their approval of us. A faithful sermon is one that declares the authority of the Bible and does so boldly.

If you're like me, you probably feel overwhelmed at this point. A faithful sermon is no small task. Crafting just one sermon that is Scripture-saturated, Christ-centered, culturally contextualized, directed to the whole person, and proclaimed boldly is beyond our own ability. We can fall short in so many ways that we may be tempted not even to start. Yet the mission is so urgent that we have to put our heads down, dig in, and do our best. My goal is to help you as you move forward. So pray that the Holy Spirit would empower you to do what you can't do on your own, and then turn the page so we can get to work.

2

MONDAY
Build the Frame

*MILESTONE: To write a clear
and concise sermon frame in two hours.*

It's Monday morning, and you may want to quit.

Yesterday you were up early. You preached with passion, answered questions, solved problems, and did your best to love and lead the people God has entrusted to you. On top of all that, if you're a church planter, you probably had to help set up and tear down equipment for your gathering. If you're anything like me, this has left you with what some call the "Holy Ghost hangover." The self-loathing started directly after you jumped into the car to drive home. You immediately started thinking about all the things you wish you would have done differently—especially in your sermon. All the things you should have said. All the things you wish you would not have said. You might be anticipating some of the emails you are likely to receive because of that one comment that slipped out. Or perhaps you know the feeling of laboring all week, preaching the best sermon you could, and then realizing *after* the sermon what the true point of the text was. If all that wasn't enough, you wake up on Monday morning under the crushing weight that you now have to do it all over again. Oh, and this is what you have chosen to do for the rest of your life.

Want to quit?

Take heart. This is what it feels like to be a preacher. Due to the spiritual, emotional, and physical ways in which preaching depletes us, Monday tends to be a discouraging, depressing, and disorienting day for many of us. All joking about quitting aside, I've heard many preachers assert that their aspiration to quit ministry is higher on Mondays than any other day of the week.

One of the best ways to refresh ourselves from the last sermon is to start the next. I'm currently in a season where I take Mondays off, but for over a decade I jumped right back in first thing Monday morning. So regardless of whether your Monday is an actual Monday or your Tuesday feels like a proverbial Monday, it's critical to get a jump on your next sermon first thing in the week rather than put it off and have it sneak up and leave you scrambling on Friday. I have found that starting my preparation early speeds up the process and produces a better sermon.

Monday's milestone is to write a clear and simple frame that the rest of the sermon will hang on—all in the course of two hours. In this chapter, we will address the place of prayer in preparation, digging into the text, reading commentary, and several aspects of writing an effective sermon frame. I break Monday's work into six steps.

1. PRAY FERVENTLY

The development and delivery of Spirit-filled, life-changing, eternity-altering sermons demands a persistent posture of prayer. We preachers are called to a task that we are incapable of accomplishing on our own. Only God can draw men and women to Himself (John 6:44). Only God can convict people of sin (John 16:8). Only God's Spirit can produce the fruit of obedience (Gal. 5:22). We are called to a task we can't do on our own. We need God's help from start to finish. This is why prayer is central to our sermon preparation. Prayer is both an acknowledgment of our dependence on God and the act of petitioning Him for help.

When we come to the task of preparation, we are wise to think of ourselves as little children dependent on a parent. My kids constantly encounter tasks they can't accomplish on their own. For instance, we have a small bounce house that they love to play in. Almost every day they beg me to set it up so they can play in it, which they do for about five minutes—until one of them bumps their head and cries frantically, leaving me looking for a match so I can burn the whole thing down to the ground. This wouldn't bother me so much if they could set it up themselves and didn't need me to do it for them. The problem is, it's simply too big for them to unpack and set up by themselves. They need my help. So they beg and beg until I give in, get it out, set it up, and . . . well, I've already told you what happens.

Our sermons are like their bounce house: they are far too big for us to handle on our own. We need our Father's help. That's where prayer comes in. We petition the Spirit of God to do what we can't do. Prayer shouldn't be relegated to just the first day of preparation. Sermon prep should look more like a perpetual prayer meeting than a seminary class. From start to finish, our eyes should be in the Book and our hearts should be turned toward heaven. Those who do this are the kind of preachers God uses.

Before we start to study, before we crack the commentary, before we write one word, we need to beg God to do what we simply can't. If you're not sure where to start, here are three things I pray over and again each week while I prep.

Father, help me understand what I'm reading. In 1 Corinthians 2:14, Paul says, "The natural person does not accept the things of the Spirit of God, for they are folly to him, and he is *not able to understand them* because they are spiritually discerned" (emphasis added). We need the Spirit of God to illuminate His Word for us. J. I. Packer defines illumination as "the applying of God's revealed truth to our hearts, so that we grasp as reality for ourselves what the sacred text sets forth."[1] Apart from the illuminating work of the Spirit, I have just as much hope of understanding the Scriptures as I do Swahili. Detaching sermon preparation from prayer is like detaching your heart from your chest—the sermon will die without it.

This is why the Puritans humbly prayed, "Help me to lift up the gates of my soul that [Christ] may come in and show me himself when I search the Scriptures, for I have no lines to fathom its depths, no wings to soar to its heights."[2] We need God's Spirit to open our eyes to see, our ears to hear, and our hearts to receive. So we start our week begging God to do what only He can do and to help us understand yet again what we're reading.

Father, help me find the sermon in the text. Just because you understand the text doesn't mean you're ready to preach it. You still need a sermon. You need a clear, concise, and compelling big idea. You need a frame or structure. You need illustrations and a helpful plan for how you will encourage people to apply whatever text you're preaching to their own lives. These few sentences alone should start to make you feel at least slightly overwhelmed. This is a lot of work. I am well acquainted with the feeling of having spent a week studying to truly understand my passage, only to have no clue what the actual sermon should be. This is why this prayer is so important.

Once we know *what* the text says, we still need God's leading to know *how* to unpack it. Like a son to his father, I come to God begging Him for help in each part of my sermon. I ask Him to help me think of and write a compelling introduction. I ask for help with my illustrations. I ask for insight into every implication that each point has for my life and the lives of those who will listen. I can't write a faithful sermon without God's help. So the only thing to do is ask for help in every part.

Father, prepare my heart to preach. The preacher's heart needs to be cultivated and prepared just like every other aspect of the sermon. Most preachers I know pray for their delivery and for the people who will be listening. But I wonder how often we pray for ourselves. We need hearts that are what and where they should be so we can say all that God has put in front of us. We need to truly love the people to whom we preach. We need to look on the crowd, regardless of its size, and be filled with Christ's compassion for it. We need to have the fear of God and not the fear of man as the rudder on the ship of our sermons. We need to have allowed these sermons to work on us before they go to work on anyone else.

These are all heart issues, and only the Holy Spirit can prepare and change hearts. So prior to anything else, begin this week of preparing yet another sermon by asking God to help you with all that you can't accomplish on your own.

While prayer can and should persist throughout the entire week, once you feel you have spent enough time in prayer on Monday morning, begin digging into the text. After prayer, your sermon starts with the text. Your preparation should not start with you trying to rip off someone else's sermon you really liked. It shouldn't start with a clever idea you want to footnote with Bible verses. It shouldn't start with a Google search for "great sermon ideas." If your sermon prep starts with something other than an open Bible and a blank page, you're doing it wrong. As we've seen, we're called to "preach the word." We don't preach our creativity, thoughts, feelings, ideas, or stories. These may be *part* of the sermon, but if they *are* the sermon, then we've wasted the time of our listeners. We're called to preach the Word, which means our preparation must start with the Scriptures themselves.

This is the part of preparation that Bible colleges and seminaries spend the most time on. We're getting into the work of exegesis. This means we're doing our best to climb into the heart and mind of the author so we can retrieve the meaning he intended for his original audience. We're doing our best, by God's grace and with the Spirit's help, to find the one interpretation and countless implications of the text we've been tasked to preach. You can find numerous books on how to interpret and then preach Scripture, so I'll keep my comments brief and specific.

2. WRITE OUT THE TEXT

Take a blank legal pad and your Bible, and start by writing out by hand whatever passage you're preaching. (The one exception I make is if I'm preaching a long narrative.) You may be tempted to skip or supplement this step in some way, but I strongly caution against it. As the popular saying goes, "Thoughts untangle themselves over the lips and through the fingertips." Writing out the biblical text forces you to slow down and thus helps you see things you would not see otherwise.

3. SEEK TO UNDERSTAND IT

To be certain you understand the flow of thought, you have to understand the words being used. At minimum, this means reading your text in multiple translations and looking up any unfamiliar words in the original language. At the risk of sounding like a salesman, I highly recommend investing in good Bible-study software. This tends to be expensive on the front end, but the investment is well worth it. When I open my Logos library and punch in my text for the week, hundreds of commentaries, lexicons, and dictionaries appear immediately. It also gives me an exegetical guide showing every word of my text in the original language. It would take hours to look up all this by hand, so if you can afford it, spend the money on the software.

4. RECORD YOUR
OBSERVATIONS AND QUESTIONS

When you write out the text and begin to understand the language that is being used, you start to see it through a fresh lens. You make connections and observations. Questions are prompted, and some are answered. Each of these is crucial to the framing of your sermon outline. Your observations may become points of insight that form the main points of your sermon. Your questions may be the same ones your listeners will have and need answers to. I consider this "interrogating the text." Before I can move on to the next step, I need to know the following (these help me further understand the text):

- Who wrote the text? What was their background and biography?
- When was the text written? Did any important historical events occur around this time?
- To whom was the text written? Were they Jews or Gentiles, or both? Where did they live? What challenges were they facing?
- What prompted the writing of this text? What is the overarching purpose of the book to which this text belongs?
- What are the key themes of this text? Are there any words repeated for emphasis?

There is no shortage of questions that can be asked and observations that can be made. Remember, at this point all you're trying to do is wade as deeply as possible into the text.

Write everything down. No detail is too small.

I once read of a seminary professor who divided his first-year Biblical Interpretations class into teams and assigned them each one verse. He told each team to work together to come up with one hundred observations on their single text. When they had finally squeezed them all out, they submitted their work to the professor, feeling relieved to have accomplished such a difficult and tedious task. The professor thanked them for their work and then gave them the follow-up assignment of taking the same verse and finding yet another hundred observations!

One thing that makes the Bible so amazing is its depth. Every text is an endless well from which to draw life-giving water. Spend the time and seize the opportunity to drink from it yourself as you prepare to feed others.

5. READ COMMENTARY

After about an hour, I've done my own work and have hopefully begun to wrap my heart and mind around the text. While we know the Holy Spirit does the work of illumination, we also know that He uses the work of other men and women to sharpen and clarify our thinking. At this point, I have my study app open, and I'm checking my own interpretation against the best commentaries I can find.

This is where many preachers lose precious time. We are blessed to live in a time and a culture where the sheer number of study resources seems endless and where the helps themselves are so easily accessible. This leads many of us to read more commentaries than we need to or have time for. Some of us are driven by a deep fear of saying anything incorrect, so we overcompensate by reading every commentary we can get our hands on. While I applaud the desire to acquire an accurate interpretation, you don't need to read everything ever written to do so. Another reason we may spend more time than we have reading commentaries is that we enjoy it. I know pastors that would rather read a commentary than do anything else.

The truth is that most of us simply don't have the time to read twenty commentaries on every passage we preach. In fact, unless you're the type of preacher who is just a teaching pastor with a sizable staff, I would not recommend that you do so. I would go so far as to argue that for most pastors, to do so would be a tragic waste of God-given time. Should you read commentary? Absolutely! Should you spend the entire week doing so? Absolutely not. You're a pastor, not just a preacher. You need to shepherd the flock God has entrusted to you. You need to spend time with people, pour into people, and train people. If you spend more time in a book than you do with Christ's bride, you're not pastoring.

Like many things in life, getting the most out of your commentaries lies in the quality, not the quantity, of what you read. You need to read the right commentaries, and that means *reading to your needs*. We all have different strengths and liabilities. Some of us are more naturally gifted when it comes to diagnosing the hearts and minds of people. Others of us were fortunate enough to go to seminary and can handle reading in the original languages. Some people are a seemingly endless well of stories and illustrations that can further serve their sermons. We all have different skills, and different commentaries meet our respective needs.

If you're weaker with the languages, you will want to read more exegetically oriented commentaries that will help you sniff out the nuances that you may have missed in your cursory reading. If you're better with books than you are with people, you may want to find good pastoral commentaries that can help you bring the text to bear on those listening to you. If you need to grow in your ability to illustrate and apply, a devotional commentary will serve you well. Self-awareness is one of the most critical skills a person can possess and develop. Do you know your strengths and weaknesses? Figure them out and read to your needs.

Clearly, there is no hard-and-fast rule on how many different commentaries you should read each week, but I typically study one in depth while skimming two or three others to supplement my more focused reading. You may have the capacity for more, but that tends to be my sweet spot.

Years ago, someone told me about BestCommentaries.com, which has proven to be a helpful site for selecting commentaries for my own personal needs. Each resource is labeled according to its intent—technical, devotional, pastoral, and so on. I tend to take the highest rated commentary on a particular book of the Bible as my primary choice and then a few more based on a combination of the author, the style of the commentary, and the commentary's rating. Your commentaries are meant to serve your preparation, not steal your time. Choose discerningly, read carefully, and pace yourself diligently. This step is only a pit stop today, as the main event starts next.

6. BUILD A SERMON FRAME

I know next to nothing about construction. My uncles are contractors and construction workers. My brother is a gifted designer and builder. Yet for some reason, the skill set necessary for building drove right past me and didn't even bother to wave. I can barely build Legos without wanting to throw them in frustration. Despite my deficient understanding of construction and architecture, I find the image of a house being built a helpful picture for sermon preparation. The house you live in hangs on a frame. The insulation, wiring, and siding that complete a home all demand that a frame be fixed in place and built properly.

Sermons are no different. A faithful sermon will hang on a frame. Our frames may take different forms, but we all need structured outlines to hold our sermons together or they will inevitably fall apart. While there are various ways to frame a sermon and various styles that preaching can take, here are my personal five commandments for framing a sermon.

Commandment 1: Thou shalt have a sermon frame. At the risk of restating the obvious, this needs to be clearly established. I have heard some preachers downplay the need for, and even discourage the use of, a sermon frame. I heard a gifted preacher once say that he does not use an outline because he does not want listeners to predict where he's going. While that may sound novel, it should not be normative.

Every sermon needs a frame—both for the preacher and for the listener. You as the preacher need to have a clear and prepared sense of where you are headed and what you are trying to say. Listeners likewise need to be able to follow you.

Preparing an outline and having a clear path does not rob them of interest. Rather, it helps them track with you. Furthermore, the likelihood that they retain points from the sermon is much higher if you have clearly framed it for them. Do not skip this step. Build a strong frame to hang your sermon on. You will preach better, and your listeners will thank you.

Commandment 2: Thou shalt have a big idea. In his Yale lectures, J. H. Jowett said, "No sermon is ready for preaching, not ready for writing out, until we can express its theme in a short, pregnant sentence as clear as a crystal."[3] *Everyone* who communicates *anything* has *something* they're trying to say. The Holy Spirit, through the human writers of Scripture, is no different. The goal of preaching is always only to say what God is saying in His Word. This means the most important part of the sermon frame must be the big idea—the one summarizing sentence that says what God is saying in any particular text. The big idea is the foundation of your frame.

You may be tempted to think, *The text I'm preaching says a lot, so my sermon is filled with lots of big ideas.* I would not dispute the fact that most texts are communicating more than one idea. Your job as the preacher, however, is to synthesize all the individual ideas into one sentence that captures the intended meaning of the author. That is your big idea, and you're not ready to preach until you have it.

Commandment 3: Thou shalt draw points from the text. There are two ways to develop the points of your sermon. One is faithful, while the other is not. The first way is to form your thoughts and ideas and then impose them onto the text. The second is to climb inside the heart and mind of the author, with the help of the Holy Spirit, and form your points from his. This is the faithful way to frame the ideas of your sermon.

Imagine you wrote someone a letter with three specific ideas you wanted to convey to them. How frustrating would it be if that person took that letter, totally disregarded what you intended, and instead imposed their own meaning and ideas upon what you wrote? None of us would want someone to do that to us. Yet this is what many of us do to God when we don't seek to understand what He's trying to convey. We certainly should never do to God, or anyone else, anything we would not want done to us. Simply put, the points of the text should be the point of your sermon. Write them in a way that is clear, compelling, and creative, but make sure they are derived from the text itself.

Commandment 4: Thou shalt keep it simple. I've seen some sermon frames that are so confusing and convoluted that they did no good. Sometimes they're confusing in their origin, in that they come from the preacher's own mind rather than the text. Other times they can be confusing in their structure—for example, when your subpoints have subpoints. Often, they can be confusing when we use words people don't understand or when we write lousy sentences.

I once preached a sermon on Luke 1:26–38 in which I used Mary as an example of what surrendering to God's will looks like. My frame looked like this:

Big Idea: To serve God is to submit to His will.
Three signs I'm surrendered to God's will . . .

1. I desire God's approval over that of all others.
2. I die to the need for all the details.
3. I believe that nothing is impossible for God.

I'm not suggesting this is the best frame ever, but it has the elements I strive for. The points are derived straight from the text and are short, simple, and memorable. Imagine if my frame looked more like this:

Big Idea: To be a servant of the Most High God like Mary will mean laying down the things we want in order to do the things God wants us to do.

1. Mary was willing to be content with the approval of God on her life over the approval of everyone around.
2. Mary would have had questions, but she did not demand every detail before she chose to trust what Gabriel said.
3. Mary was willing to take God at His Word and believe that there was nothing He could not do.

Both frames communicate essentially the same content. The second could actually be far more confusing than it is. What makes the first more helpful is how simple it is. There are no wasted words. Faithful preaching always strives for clarity, and that means laboring for simplicity.

Simplicity can get a bad rap. Sometimes we mistakenly believe that because something is simple, it must be watered down. Many of us prefer complexity because it makes us feel more intelligent and appear more impressive. Admittedly, a simple sermon frame can be reductionistic if we strip away essential aspects of the text's meaning in the name of saying something simple. To be sure, that is not what I'm vying for.

What I want to do every week is work through complexity until I arrive at simplicity. A faithful sermon frame distills the complex down to its simple and essential components. Your listeners should not need a PhD to follow your sermon. At the risk of offending you, which is not my intention, it needs to be said: confusing preaching is the result of laziness. If your sermon is confusing, it means you haven't worked diligently enough on behalf of your listeners. Don't settle for something only you can understand. Work through complexity to arrive at simplicity. God will be honored, and your church will be served well.

Commandment 5: Thou shalt commit to completing it early. You may feel prone to push back, thinking, *It's only Monday. Why would I put pressure on myself to finish my sermon outline this early in the week?* That's a fair question. The answer is that it will help you prepare a better sermon. You and I are laboring together to write faithful sermons faster. Remember, the idea of writing your sermon in eight hours or less is about the time you spend at the desk. If you're a preacher, you're always preparing a sermon. Getting a good jump on your outline allows you to sit on it longer while you soak up everything you hear, see, and experience throughout the week. You may read stories, have conversations, and make observations throughout the week that will greatly aid the clarity of your sermon. But you can't do that if you don't know early on where you're headed. What you want to establish early in the week is the general direction you're headed. Your frame may evolve over the course of the week, so don't feel like you have to have everything nailed down on Monday. You're simply trying to avoid leaving everything until the last minute.

It's time to get to work. Pray fervently. Write out the text. Seek to understand it. Record your observations and questions. Read commentary. And construct a clear and simple frame to build the rest of your sermon on. Remember, there's nothing magical about the two-hour mark. It's a goal, not a rule. This process will take time to develop, and you will get faster as you continue. Don't be discouraged if you get to the two-hour mark and are not finished. Work the process and don't waste time. Each week you will get better, until in due time you become the most efficient version of yourself. You're not alone in this. God is with you, and every faithful preacher of God's Word is doing the same thing you are. Let's lean in and get after it together.

3

TUESDAY
Open the Door

---

*MILESTONE: To finalize the sermon
frame with a team in one hour.*

I've been an athlete most of my life, which means I've spent my fair share of time in a gym. I know the sound of weights being racked. I know the combined smell of sweat and insecurity that fills most fitness centers. I know the sight of muscle heads walking around proudly, wearing T-shirts that appear to have been cut with a Weedwacker, while carrying gallon-sized jugs of water like they are preparing to walk across the desert and may never see liquid again.

In all my years of going to the gym, there is one day— one guy, really—I will never forget. He walked in like a fighter entering the ring. He had this air about him, like he thought everyone was there for him, like the staff had turned on "Welcome to the Jungle" because it was his walk-in music. Despite his confidence, I'm pretty sure I'm the only one who noticed him. Upon entering, he walked directly to the throne of strength in every gym—the bench press. He proceeded to load the bar with more weight than I'd ever seen anyone press. With every plate he loaded, he looked around the room as if he were thinking, *Can you guys believe I'm going to lift this much?* Still, nobody was watching him.

Once the bar was loaded, the sideshow of psyching himself up began. There was grunting and snorting. There was the occasional self-pep talk of "You got this!" From what I could tell, it was far more pageantry than true preparation. After this circus was over, it was finally time for the moment we had all been waiting for—actually just me, because nobody else was watching. He lay down on the bench, grasped the bar like he was going to teach it a lesson it would never forget, gave himself one last pep talk, and pushed the bar off the rack.

It took only a second to see this was about to go bad in the worst way possible. Every muscle in his body began to shake as he started to slowly lean to the left. I don't know exactly what was running through his head, but somewhere in the mix must have been, *Oh my gosh, I put way too much weight on, and it's too late to remedy!* On the upside, he was about to have what he had wanted since he walked in—the undivided attention of everyone in the gym. As he leaned farther and farther, the first plate slipped off and fell to the floor, alerting everyone of the train wreck happening. This began a teeter-tottering back and forth of the bar as he dropped every plate he had loaded.

Before you become too concerned about this guy's personal welfare, the only thing wounded in the incident was his pride.

If you frequent a gym, you've probably seen this, or something similar, happen before. It's the result of overassuming one's own ability and underutilizing the strength of the people around you. All this guy had to do was ask someone to spot him, and the embarrassing and potentially dangerous fiasco would never have happened.

Sadly, many preachers make the same sort of mistake. The task of preaching can feel like a crushing weight, especially when you have to do it week after week. For nearly my first decade of preaching, I carried this weight alone. Every sermon was my personal Everest that I was intent on conquering alone. This resulted in many subpar sermons and in stress levels that were unsustainable for me. It took me longer than it needed to, but I finally learned that, while we cannot delegate the task of sermon prep to someone else, we can draw others into the process for the purpose of helping us produce better sermons under less stress. This is what gave birth to my weekly group prep meeting.

I started gathering several people together around a whiteboard every Tuesday so I could walk them through my sermon frame. This started as a way to ensure everything I wanted to say made sense. To my surprise, I walked away with much more than I had planned—helpful illustrations, fresh insights into how people may receive the sermon, and content that was far more compelling than what I had generated alone. My hope is that you might try this and discover similar benefits. Let's start with the goals of a group prep meeting.

THE GOALS
OF A GROUP PREP MEETING

To ensure you're saying what the text says. The first thing I want to ensure is that I'm being faithful to the biblical text. It's important that the point of the text be the point of my sermon. Hopefully you have already done your own exegetical work and read commentary, but you're still human and capable of mistakes. We've all had the experience of believing we understood something only to have someone else dismantle what we thought we knew.

This happened to me every week in my college literature class. Every week the class would discuss the book we had read, and every week I went in thinking I understood it. As my professor and classmates started to debate and dialogue about the point of view, the characters, and the plot line, I quickly felt that I had read the wrong book because my understanding was so far off from what was being discussed. I'd love to say I got better as the semester went on, but instead I just went back to reading cheap, poorly written crime novels.

Hopefully we're not this far from the meaning of the biblical text. But even if we miss something, we need to learn of it prior to stepping into the pulpit. Sitting with a group of people and talking them through how you landed where you did places another level of protection around you.

To ensure your thoughts make sense. Sometimes our thoughts are not as clear as they seem in our heads. Furthermore, as a preacher, your thoughts need to be clear not only to you, but also to those listening to you. Just because something makes sense in your head doesn't mean it will necessarily make sense to others. Marriage has taught me this time and again. If I had a dollar for every conversation I had with my wife when I thought I was making a crystal clear, even irrefutable, point, only to have her stare blankly at me—well, let's just say I wouldn't still be driving my 2002 Ford Explorer.

The group prep meeting is the first chance to filter your thoughts through the ears of other people. You will either see clarity in their eyes, or they'll squint politely at you, in hopes of not having to tell you they have no clue what you're getting at. Either way it's a win. We're after a clear, concise, and compelling sermon, so open the door and let other people help you ensure you're headed in that direction.

To ensure you have considered the state of your listeners. The main reason I prepare with a group is to help me think about how best to communicate the text to the various types of people in our church. Preachers tend to spend all their time exegeting the text and little to no time exegeting their people. This is the reason for many subpar sermons. The preacher's task is to bring the text to bear on the lives of those listening. You simply cannot do that if you don't know who they are. What are the dominant worldviews held by people in your church? What are their theological presuppositions? What is their level of biblical literacy? What are their struggles, doubts, and difficulties? What implications does the text have for teenagers, college students, newly married couples, single parents, widows, or elderly people? You can't know the answers to these questions if you sit in your study with lexicons and commentaries forty hours a week. You have to spend time with the people you pastor, and one way to take steps in that direction is to gather a few of those people together and talk through your sermon with them.

Now that we're clear on what we're trying to accomplish in a group prep meeting, let's talk about how to structure the meeting.

TIPS FOR A
PRODUCTIVE GROUP PREP MEETING

Get the right people. For this time to be productive, you need to have the right people present. First, they should be people you know and trust. This is a vulnerable time in the life of your sermon. Submitting partially formed thoughts and ideas to a group of people is nerve-racking. You may be only partially convinced that your thoughts make sense and that you are headed in the right direction, so it can be difficult to allow other people to evaluate your sermon. This is why it's important to meet with people you know and trust. You need to be confident they are for you and truly want to help you write the best sermon possible.

Second, it's important that they know your church. This is so they can help you process the sermon through the eyes and ears of others. I can't overstate the importance of exegeting the people who make up your church. This is more natural for some than for others. If you're naturally relational and read people well, this may come naturally for you. If you're not, it is especially important for you to empower others to help you grow in this discipline. Grab another pastor, small group leader, ministry team leader, or someone else who is well connected to the life of your church. Ask them to process what you're explaining through the eyes and ears of others in the church. Over time, you will become increasingly adept at exegeting your people. People will think you're a prophet, when in truth you just pay attention and know the people to whom you are preaching.

Third, try to use the same people every week if possible. The more you gather as a group, the more you will slip into a rhythm and grow in chemistry. You'll have less awkward pauses, fewer confused looks, and better ideas being generated. If the group you work with changes every week, it will feel like you are starting over time and again. If you're worried about inviting someone who proves not to be a good fit, then simply invite everyone to help you with an experiment. Don't pose it as a meeting that they must sign up for forever or not attend at all. It's easier not to invite someone to a meeting again than to remove them from a team. Keep it low-key and find the right people prior to solidifying a team.

Make sure you are ready. I do not recommend starting your sermon prep with a group. You need to have done your work and have at least written a rough sermon frame prior to sorting through it with others. You're the one who is going to preach it, so it is critical you understand both the text and the direction you're headed. I've found I need to have my frame 90 percent complete prior to my group prep meeting or else the meeting tends to be a waste of time.

Most importantly, this means knowing exactly what you're looking for from the team. Is there a point for which you need better language? Is there an application you want them to help you think through? Is there an illustration you're not sure is clear? Have all this sorted out prior to your meeting so you can tell them what you're looking for. If you have the right people, they will want to be helpful, but they won't know how to be if you don't tell them what you need.

Walk them through the sermon. It's amazing how talking through your sermon in this early stage begins to embed it deep into your heart and mind. It also begins to untangle your thoughts. Open your time with prayer, asking God for clarity and wisdom, read your text, and then walk them through what you see and where you're headed in the sermon. If I already have an idea for the introduction, then I start there. Otherwise, I simply begin with the main points of my sermon frame. It may feel uncomfortable at first due to the fact that you're still trying to sort it all out in your own head, but this can help you refine your own thoughts.

Don't resist constructive criticism. Your posture and response to people's feedback will determine whether or not they feel the freedom to actually dialogue with you and thus be helpful. Give them permission to ask questions and to poke holes in your reasoning. Most importantly, don't respond defensively when they do. Make no mistake, as people sit and listen to your sermon on Sunday morning, they're doing the same thing. The only difference is that you can't hear them on Sunday because they're doing it in their heads. Talking through your sermon with other people prior to preaching helps you anticipate questions, objections, and areas of confusion. Tell everyone at the outset that you welcome critical feedback, and then respond with humility and gratitude when they provide it.

If you're still not convinced of the value of drawing others into your process, let me offer you four advantages to opening the door.

ADVANTAGES TO
GROUP PREP MEETINGS

Sharing the load makes the work go faster. You've probably spent hours on your own trying to think of an illustration, a necessary cross-reference, or even just one word to clarify an idea you want to communicate. On occasion, this is simply part of the price of being a preacher, but it need not be the norm. When even just two or three other people put their heads together and help you look for elements like these, not only does it lighten your load, but it also helps you find what you need faster.

I have three little kids who lose their stuff constantly. A toy car, a baby doll, a blanket—something always seems to be lost. If Tami and I left our kids to find everything on their own, it would take them days. Instead, we spend the better part of most days helping them find whatever they're looking for. Except on rare occasions, we can usually find whatever they've lost in a matter of minutes. Searching together speeds up the process.

The same is true in sermon prep. There is no advantage in trying to solve every problem, answer every question, or generate every idea on your own. Weekly sermon prep is brutal all on its own. We don't need to make it even more difficult by insisting on doing everything in a vacuum. Open the door, draw others into your preparation process, and watch how much faster it moves forward.

Sharing the load produces a better end product. Remember, we are not simply after speed and efficiency. Anyone can crank out a lousy sermon in a few hours. There's no skill in

59

that. We're after more: *faithful* sermons and *better* sermons. The best ideas typically stem from the mind of a group rather than one person. The germ of a sermon element always starts in one mind, but a second idea from another almost always makes it stronger. Nearly every week at the end of my group prep meeting, I look at the whiteboard, and it's filled with ideas, thoughts, and insights that I did not have on my own prior to the meeting. Every week I think, *This is so much better than what I had an hour ago.* The truth is either you will not come up with these ideas at all if left to yourself or it will take you exponentially longer to do so.

Sharing the load protects you from mistakes. You're not perfect. You are capable of exegetical mistakes and pastoral insensitivities. If you're investing time in reading this book, I can't imagine that you are careless and have no concern about making such mistakes. But they can still happen because preachers are human. Inviting more minds to the process and putting more eyes on the sermon provides you with another safeguard against mistakes.

I want someone to speak up on a Tuesday morning and say, "I don't think point number two says what the text says." Receiving that sort of remark on Tuesday is far better than getting one of those painful emails on Monday morning telling me a similar thing—only about the sermon I preached the day before. Often you can't fix mistakes once you've preached them. So try to catch them before you preach. I could give you endless examples of things I had planned to say but did not because someone helped me see the way it could be received. Such feedback is a gift. You can either humble yourself on the front end, asking others for insight, or you can be humiliated on the back end when someone brings the already-preached mistake to your attention. Choose to fix it on the front end.

Sharing the load prepares others to preach. A by-product of drawing others into the preparation process is that it gives younger preachers with less experience more insight into how you develop a sermon. They get to see the thought that goes into it. They get to see how it holds together. They get to hear you wrestle with the text and see the value of laboring to get it right. Sermon prep should not be some mysterious process understood by only a select few. You're not Harry Potter, and sermon prep isn't magic. It is a craft, a process people can replicate.

REASONS WE DON'T OPEN THE DOOR

While I can think of many advantages to inviting others into your preparation, I can't think of any advantages of *not* doing so. I am, however, aware of a few obstacles that may keep us from this step.

Pride: I need to do this alone. When I first started preaching, I had a deep desire to be some strange version of Moses coming down the mountain with a word from God. I wanted to be locked away in my study by myself and emerge on Sunday with a powerful sermon that God would use to transform lives. What I did not want was to rely on others for help. I loved serving the church with others, but the sermon needed to be *my* work.

The truth is that I wanted to impress people. I wish I could say this desire has faded over time, but if I'm honest, I still want to impress people, and my guess is you do, too. This desire is fueled by pride. First Peter 5:5 reminds us that

"God opposes the proud but gives grace to the humble." Think about that. If your preparation is permeated with pride, the God you're supposed to proclaim is opposing you in the process! But if we're humble, God promises us grace—and there's nothing you and I need more than grace.

One of the most helpful ways we can humble ourselves is by opening the study door and inviting a few other people in to help us. If they catch something that needs correction, listen. If someone else has a better idea, use it. If something you think is clever lacks clarity, fix it. You can't lose with humility—ever. You're not Moses, and neither am I. So let's open the door and fill our preparation with strong minds and humble hearts.

Opportunity: I don't have anyone who can help me. If you're a church planter or a solo pastor with no staff, you may be tempted to believe this is something you can do only if you have an office full of people working with you, but that's simply not true. Almost anyone can help you during your preparation. Remember, one of the main goals of group preparation is to filter your sermon frame through the ears of those who will listen to you preach. You're trying to anticipate any objections, questions, and points of confusion that may arise. This means that anyone in your church can be of service. You don't need people with preaching experience, theological degrees, or even tremendous spiritual maturity. Your church is filled with people from different walks of life, with various presuppositions, and at various points in their discipleship journeys. Ideally you can pull together a small group of people who represent the diversity of your congregation. Even if that is too much too fast, you'll be amazed at what you can accomplish if you find just one person in your church you trust, take them out for coffee, and talk them through your sermon. I simply don't believe that you don't have people who can help you. Take a chance, invite a few friends, and try it out.

Ignorance: I have never even thought of this. Maybe it's not pride or an apparent lack of people keeping you from involving others. Perhaps it's the sheer fact that it has never crossed your mind. Maybe no one has ever encouraged you to consider this. Maybe you are like I was and have been gutting it out alone for a while now, and this is the first time you've ever considered the idea. I had a similar experience in my personal fitness.

I remember the first time I read about high-intensity interval training (HIIT), an exercise strategy that involves alternating short bursts of intense anaerobic exercise (e.g., sprints, burpees, box jumps, kettle bell swings—pretty much anything that feels like it may kill you) with less intense recovery periods. Essentially, you alternate from feeling like you're going to puke, pass out, or die to short periods of relief. I'd been exercising most of my life, but I'd been doing it similar to the guy I opened the chapter with. I'd do a bench press set, sit around for a few minutes, then do another. When I started doing more HIIT workouts, I wondered why I had done anything else. I found it to be much more effective and efficient, and *it took someone telling me about it* for me to give it a try. That's what I'm praying this chapter does for you.

I'm not aware of many preaching books that encourage this practice. I also don't believe it's being taught regularly in seminaries and Bible colleges. This is unfortunate. The lack of knowledge about this limits many preachers from preparing the best sermons they possibly can in the least amount of time.

My hope is that you will try this. What do you have to lose? All it takes is an hour. In fact, if you let it run longer, you're wasting time. Get in the text, spend a couple hours hammering out your rough frame, then open the door and invite a few people in to help you finalize it. It may just be the single greatest discipline you develop.

4

WEDNESDAY
Sweat the Intro

MILESTONE: To write in one hour an introduction that will grab people's attention.

A pastor once told me, "If you open strong, hit your transitions, and land the plane well, your sermon will take care of itself." While I've found it to be slightly more complicated than that, he was largely correct. Most sermons will fall apart before they even start due to poor openings, create confusion due to sloppy transitions, or crash and burn because of an inability to "land the plane." No one could follow along even if they wanted to.

The problem is that many preachers worry solely about getting the text right, but there is more to a faithful sermon than the text. You can get the text right and still get the sermon wrong. Now before you burn my book because it seems like I don't care about getting the text right, take a breath. You have to get the text right. In fact, if you get everything else right, but you get the text wrong, nothing else matters. If you miss the text, you're not a preacher; you're just a communicator. The world has enough communicators. What it needs is preachers. And faithful preachers are Word-centered. Our chief goal is to faithfully communicate God's Word to God's people with the help of God's Spirit. All that to say, hopefully you and I are back on the same page and you no longer believe I am a heretic. Now back to my original point: you can get the text right and still get the sermon wrong.

Most "train-wreck" sermons I've had the unfortunate experience of sitting through have been absolutely faithful to the text. The problem is, preaching is about being faithful not only to the text but also to the listener. Faithfulness to your listeners demands many things, the first of which is a strong introduction to your sermon.

There are essentially two kinds of preachers: those who sweat the introduction and those who hardly care about it. The latter will simply announce their text, spew a series of sentences that have no true connection to the sermon, and maybe pray. (After all, can it really be a sermon if you don't pray before you preach it?)

Thankfully, other preachers do sweat the intro. You know them when you hear them. They're the ones you can tell have labored to find common ground with their listeners and seek to draw them in with a toolbox full of creative ways to grab their attention. A good introduction grabs people by the face and demands they listen—metaphorically speaking, of course. If you literally grab a listener's face, you may end up in jail for assault, which I imagine would be a downer for everyone involved.

Grabbing the attention of listeners has never been more necessary than it is now in our culture. People come into our worship services each week already inundated with information. They're weighed down by the stress of their own lives and perhaps distracted by something they heard on the news. And before they walked through the church door, they most likely were listening to music, checking Twitter and Facebook, posting to Instagram—you name it. A good introduction will cut through the noise of distractions and tell listeners why they should pay attention to what you have to say. If you don't accomplish this in the first five minutes, you may have lost the battle already. Capturing attention needs to happen quickly.

TOOLS FOR WRITING
EFFECTIVE INTRODUCTIONS

Writing a strong introduction isn't easy. It requires thoughtful, prayerful intentionality. The good news is there are some proven tools at our disposal for creating effective sermon introductions. I will keep my list to five.

Tension

My guess is we've all played tug-of-war at some point in our lives, maybe at recess, in gym class, or at a picnic. One team grabs the end of a rope, and the opposing team takes the other end. Both teams then tug until one is pulled across a line, into a mud puddle, or through some other unfortunate and typically messy substance.

Tug-of-war is a game of tension. Tension is the state

of being stretched tight, and as a preacher, it's an effective means of grabbing your listeners' attention. When people are stretched tight emotionally and mentally, you'd better believe they're paying attention. Tension is uncomfortable, and people pay attention to what makes them uncomfortable. The question is, how do we create tension in preaching?

One way is to uncover the particular problem your sermon will solve. Tension is the time and space between what should be and what actually is. If you were to listen to almost any sermon I have preached in the last few years, at some point in my introduction you would hear me say, "The problem is . . . ," and then follow that with a clearly stated problem common to everyone listening. Here are a few examples I've used in the past:

Here's a problem we face today: failure to follow God's plan guarantees we forfeit the fight.

God promises to renew the strength of those who rely on Him. Our problem is we often don't know why we're so worn out and honestly just don't follow God's way forward.

Here's our problem this morning: each of us is prone to believe lies about Jesus that run the risk of ruining our relationship *with* Him, tanking our trust *in* Him, and destroying our dependence *on* Him.

Here's the universal problem we all face: We're all born into this world hopelessly lost. The Bible tells us—and our experience confirms—that there is no part of our being that has not been touched and polluted by sin.

Here's the problem: When you sand the edges of Scripture, you strip the message God has communicated. God's communicating something in the discomfort. He has a message in the messiness. He's telling us something about His character in the chaos we see in Scripture. So if we sand the edges off, we strip the message.

I choose to address tension directly because sometimes we have to help people face a reality they don't know or don't want to believe exists. Humans have an impressive and unfortunate ability to convince themselves that things are far better than they truly are.

Thankfully, preaching is all about truth. Faithful preaching won't let listeners live in some fictional neverland where everything is okay all the time. Instead, faithful preaching demands that listeners face the fact that everyone has been fundamentally flawed since the fall. Tension is what people feel when we take them to this place.

The general problem we should push people to is the inevitable reality that we struggle to believe and obey virtually everything the Bible tells us. There's a divide between what is and what should be—that's the tension. And even if it's not the result of our own sin, it can be caused by sin in general or the sin of others against us. My goal is to immediately help people see a specific pain point they may be ignorant of and then help them lean into the reality of the tension it causes.

Humor

Few things are more disarming yet more dangerous than humor. Humor is disarming because most people love to laugh. (I say "most" because I know a few crabby Christians who would greatly benefit from a few more chuckles now and then.) Yet humor is dangerous because it can be easily abused. In the course of one sentence, humor can cease being productive and instead make you look foolish—or worse, it can distract your listeners from the true importance of what you're trying to communicate.

While some disagree, I believe the power of humor makes it a tool worth using, but let me offer a few precautions. Not everyone is funny. God has given us different personalities, and we should preach from the personality God has seen fit to give us. Martin Luther and Charles Spurgeon were funny men who used humor as an effective communication tool. Other preachers are not particularly funny and wisely don't use humor in their preaching. If your favorite preacher is funny, it doesn't mean you should try to be. If you're not naturally funny, don't try to be something you're not. There are few things more awkward than having to give someone a pity laugh, so don't put people in that position.

Also, don't use humor if it doesn't fit the subject matter. Opening a sermon on suffering by telling a joke or light-hearted story is insensitive at best. The tone of the text should inform the tools we use. At times, humor is the perfect way to connect with the hearts and minds of those listening. At other times, however, nothing could be less appropriate. You have to discern the difference.

Finally, don't use humor for the sake of humor. Preachers

are not stand-up comedians. We are heralds of good news. I've always loved to make people laugh, and that can be a liability for me as a preacher. I have to constantly ask myself why I'm chasing the laugh. If it's to serve the greater goal of grabbing attention so I can convey something of eternal significance, then great. If it's serving my own selfish desire to hear people laugh at something I've said, I need to repent and run a different route.

Many approach preaching as though laughter were at odds with the serious nature of the subject matter we preach. I agree that humor isn't always appropriate, but it's not always inappropriate. Ecclesiastes 3:4 reminds us that there is indeed "a time to laugh." If you're funny and the humor fits the subject matter, I believe even the sermon can be a time to laugh.

When appropriate, I'll regularly use a funny personal story or observation to draw people in. Laughter has a way of making people drop their guard and can be used to land a strategic proverbial punch to the nose of those listening. Know yourself, play to your strengths, and use humor carefully.

Controversy

There is little I find more captivating than listening to someone discuss a controversial topic. For me, the fact that everything in our culture is so sanitized and politically correct makes it refreshing to hear someone with courage say what needs to be said.

The Bible has become increasingly controversial as our culture has become increasingly secularistic. The exclusivity of Christ, marriage as the union of one man and one woman, sex reserved for marriage, loving your enemies, gender roles

—the Bible is filled with content that runs contrary to the opinions of our culture. While this is a heartbreaking reality we live with, it can be used to our advantage as preachers. Controversy is engaging. What better way to grab people's attention than to lean into the controversy in the text?

Read that last sentence again. I said we should lean into the controversy *in the text*. I'm not saying the church needs you and me to be "shock jocks." I'm not arguing that we be controversial for the sake of controversy. You're probably aware of pastors who seem to create controversy just to create controversy, but this is a far cry from what I'm calling for. Like everything in the sermon, any controversy we lean into should be text driven. We need not say any more or any less than what is actually in the text.

The secret is that there is always something controversial in the text. As we discussed in chapter 1, a faithful sermon always preaches Christ. The gospel always has been and always will be controversial. In 1 Corinthians 1:18, Paul said, "For the word of the cross is folly to those who are perishing." All you have to do is tell people they were created by God and have forsaken Him, that they stand under His righteous wrath and need to trust in the sinless life, substitutionary death, and victorious resurrection of Jesus in order to be saved, and you should have people's attention. It is difficult to be more controversial than that in our day.

Using controversy well requires preparation and practice. If we do it right, our listeners may not always agree with the text, but they certainly will listen.

Story

Everyone enjoys a good story. This is why we love books, good television, and movies. Stories draw us in; they capture our focus and demand our attention. That's why so many people binge watch TV shows. Tami and I were mildly obsessed with the show *Lost* when it was still airing. This was prior to Netflix, so when a new season was released, we would rent it disk by disk from Blockbuster. We would hurry home, put in the first disk, and jump on the couch. The next thing we knew it was one o'clock in the morning and pitch-black outside. We still had tasks to accomplish, jobs to do, and sleep to catch, but the story had sucked us in so much that we forgot about it all.

As humbling as it may be, people will often remember the good stories we tell more than the carefully crafted sentences we write. When I talk to people in my church, they often reference my stories; they seldom refer to a point from my sermon, a big idea, or some phrase I labored tediously to construct. I don't think this necessarily means I'm a lousy preacher (I'll leave that for you to decide). I think it simply reinforces that stories are powerful. They get our attention, keep our attention, and, when they're effective, stay in our minds.

This means we should grow in our understanding of how to tell stories well. We should be collectors of quality stories that can be used down the road. We should study those who are best at storytelling. We shouldn't just consume quality storytelling, but we should also seek to understand what makes for good storytelling. If you can tell a good story that fits your text or introduces your topic, people will be anxious to hear more.

Confrontation

It is difficult to be indifferent when confronted. When someone gets in your face about something, you have no choice but to pay attention. I believe faithful preachers have to get in the face of their people sometimes. I'm not suggesting we yell, bully, or use harsh language. Rather, I'm suggesting that we love God's people enough to say hard things to them. Love that remains silent on issues that may cause listeners pain if left unaddressed is no love at all. True love tells the truth even when it's confrontational.

You will grab people's attention if you step up to the pulpit and in your intro make confrontational claims such as these:

I want to start this morning by addressing the fact that oftentimes we struggle to truly trust God.

We all aspire to be served and avert serving others sacrificially.

Many of us want a word *from* God but aren't willing to invest time in the Word *of* God.

Before you head into the pulpit like a bully with a bat this weekend, here are two words of caution concerning when *not* to use confrontation.

You should not confront people you don't care about. In my experience, people welcome hard words when they come from a soft heart. People aren't stupid. They can feel our heart toward them more than we think. If your heart toward the people you preach to is not loving, they will know.

You may push back, thinking, *I'm a pastor. I obviously love and care about my people.* While that may be true, I've been a pastor long enough to know that many motives drive men to ministry, and love for people is not always one of them. Some men just want a platform. Some men want authority, power, or the respect they believe comes with the responsibility of pastoral leadership. I pray that this is not you, but it is worth examining your motives.

One of the most important devotional exercises for a pastor is to find a quiet and private space where you can ask the Holy Spirit to help you discern your heart toward your church. Peter said, "Above all, keep loving one another earnestly, since love covers a multitude of sins" (1 Peter 4:8). This applies to pastors, too. Above all, we are to love the people God has entrusted to us. If you receive feedback that you're too harsh, such feedback may be directed less at what you say and more toward how you say it. You may be saying the right things from the wrong heart. If you love the people you preach to, they will love you back for saying hard things to them. Sure, some people harden their hearts to the conviction of the Spirit and will be angry or offended no matter what you say or how you say it. But let's not let that minority prevent us from doing the difficult work of ensuring our hearts are motivated by love in all things. Check your heart and be certain you deeply care about the people you must confront.

You should not confront people you don't have capital with. A good pastor has to keep his finger on the pulse of his people. Relationships, like everything else in life, work according to an economy. Encouragement and time are deposits into our relationships, and things like confrontation are withdrawals.

Both are necessary, but you have to make sure you have the capital before you make the withdrawal. As I write this, I am only a few months into my pastorate at a new church. There was a way I could say something at Redemption Bible Church, which I planted and pastored for seven years, that I shouldn't yet say in a new place to new people because I haven't built the relational capital I need in order to do so.

Confrontation is effective but should be used sparingly. Remember, your job is to faithfully feed people a weekly meal from the Word that will bear fruit in their lives. Sometimes that will mean confronting issues directly. As the saying goes, when you're a hammer, everything looks like a nail. You're not a hammer; you're a pastor, which means everyone should look like a sheep in need of a shepherd. Love and serve them well.

TIPS FOR WRITING
EFFECTIVE INTRODUCTIONS

Set your own schedule. I've read advice saying you should save the writing of your introduction until the end of your sermon prep, but I haven't been able to do that. There is a concern that if you write your intro too early in the process, it—rather than the text—may drive the direction of your sermon. I would argue that if you have nailed down a text-centered big idea and have written a clear outline, you are fine to write the intro early on. I try to develop an introduction that contains a theme I then seek to weave throughout the entire sermon. If I wait until my sermon is written, I can't do that well. Rather than build an ironclad rule regarding when you should write your intro, I simply want to say this: do what works for you.

Write an intro that fits the tone of the biblical text. This is worth stating again: the text should determine the tone of the sermon. A sermon on the suffering of Christ should sound different than a sermon on stewardship. Telling a funny story about my kids and trying to draw listeners in with humor on a day I'm preaching on human suffering will come across as insensitive at best and unloving at worst. The way you start will inform the way people think and feel their way through the sermon. Make sure your intro matches the tone of the text.

Keep it tight. No one likes to listen to a preacher drone on about everything he's going to say. Listeners don't need to hear every statistic from every study that's been conducted on a topic. They don't need three stories when one will suffice. They don't need an exhaustive archaeological lesson to help them understand the setting of the people to whom the biblical text was written. Keep your introduction tight. Abraham Lincoln's famous Gettysburg Address was only 701 words and would have taken only six or seven minutes to deliver. Those few minutes changed the trajectory of America. What matters is not how long your sermon and intro are but that you grab the attention of your listeners.

Introductions matter more than we tend to think. Your intro gets everyone on the bus and in the right seat for the journey God's called you to take them on.

It's Wednesday, and you have one hour. Hopefully you've been thinking about it since Monday. Sit down, set a timer, and write something that will grab people's attention and hold on to it for the remainder of the sermon.

5

THURSDAY
Land the Plane

MILESTONE: To write a
Christ-centered conclusion in one hour.

I'm not a huge fan of flying. It has nothing to do with the fear of crashing. I simply find it uncomfortable. To start, you have to squeeze into a tiny seat apparently designed by and for elves. I'm not even tall, but my knees still end up being planted firmly into the back of whomever has the displeasure of sitting in front of me. Then, for some reason that I will never understand, it always seems to be hot—like surface-of-the-sun hot. The first thing I do every time I board a plane is twist that tiny knob that kicks out just enough recycled air to make the experience tolerable. Yet why does the air turn off every time the plane backs out of the gate? It doesn't exactly give me confidence in the aircraft when they can't figure out how to both drive in reverse and have the air conditioning running.

I'm very much aware of what a diva I am. I know God could have put me in a time when humans traveled by covered wagon—or camel, even. If sitting in a cramped seat and being cooked on an aircraft are my greatest travel discomforts, I have it pretty good. Still, my favorite part of every flight is when the captain or flight attendant announces that the plane has begun its descent.

Just like a flight, every sermon needs to land. I'm sure you're a good preacher and that people enjoy listening to you, but they don't want to forever. They want to go home eventually. At the right time and in the right way, you have to bring your sermon to a close. If it's going to have maximum effect, the sermon needs to land clearly, smoothly, and in a timely fashion. Sadly, many poor sermons start strong and are stained when they fail to conclude well. The challenge is to prevent the many ways a sermon can crash and burn.

To be honest, this is one of the areas of preaching I struggle with the most. Landing has always been difficult for me. A few years ago, I started noticing that my conclusions were lacking, and I determined that it was because I never wrote them until the end of my preparation. I was worn out from a solid week of preparation, so I inevitably ended up slapping together the conclusion at the last minute. To combat this, I shifted the timing of when I wrote them. Rather than limping across the finish line late Friday or throwing something together Sunday morning, I started writing my conclusion on Thursday. This ensured I was fresh when writing it and helped me know exactly where I was headed.

Sometimes I'm not totally sure where I'm going to end

up and can't complete it until Friday. But as long as I have a clear frame, I typically have a sense of where I'm trying to end up. My goal in this chapter is to highlight some of the ways sermons can crash and burn in the close, share a few tips for writing a strong, Christ-centered conclusion, and invite you to experiment with writing your close earlier in the week.

HOW TO CRASH AND BURN

You may be tempted to disregard the importance of the conclusion, but people have a tendency to remember the last thing you say more than the first. This means the conclusion can hold a disproportionate amount of weight. When we crash and burn, it negatively impacts what might be an otherwise great sermon. Don't rest on the laurels of one good point or a well-crafted big idea. We want every second of the sermon to be our absolute best, including our closing words. So here are the three most common ways to crash the close of a sermon.

Circling without a Clear Spot to Land

Have you ever been on a flight when there was bad weather at your destination? Often when this happens, the plane has to circle the airport until conditions are conducive for the plane to land. The only thing that sets me on edge more than flying is being on a plane for several hours and then circling the airport, knowing that we can't land quite yet.

Sadly, I've sat through more than one sermon that feels the same way. Equally sad is that I've preached more than one sermon that feels the same way. Sometimes we go round and round, reiterating our points, restating our big idea, and recommunicating our entire sermon, while we look over the side hoping to find some place to "land the plane." Meanwhile, people are thinking, *This was all fine the first time I heard it, but when is he going to finish?*

This is always an issue of preparation. When you head into the pulpit without a clearly defined destination, you simply haven't been thoughtful enough in your preparation. Maybe your strategy has simply been to "let the Spirit lead" as you close. That's a bad strategy. Not the "let-the-Spirit-lead" part, but the failure to see that the Spirit leads our preparation and not just the act of preaching. Let the Spirit lead your conclusion and every other part of your sermon. Let Him lead you in the study and not just on the stage.

Landing without Presenting Christ

The evangelist D. L. Moody spent the evening of Sunday, October 8, 1871, the way he spent many other Sunday nights: preaching. His text was Matthew 27:22, and his topic was What shall we do then with Jesus which is called Christ? On the surface, this was a night like many others. But Moody made a decision that was different and that diverged from his normal practice. Rather than concluding with an appeal for people to put their faith in Jesus, Moody said, "I wish you would take this text home with you and turn it over in your minds during the week, and the next Sabbath we will come to Calvary and the cross, and we will decide what to do with Jesus of Nazareth."[1] This decision to send people home to "turn it over" in their minds would hang over Moody's head for the rest of his ministry.

As they sang their closing song, the fire alarms sounded.

The Great Chicago Fire had broken out, killing 300 people and leaving more than 10,000 homeless. This tragic event proved to be a turning point in Moody's ministry. He later said,

> I have never since dared to give an audience a week to think of their salvation. If they were lost they might rise up in judgment against me. I have never seen that congregation since. I will never meet those people until I meet them in another world. But I want to tell you of one lesson that I learned that night which I have never forgotten, and that is, when I preach, to press Christ upon the people then and there and try to bring them to a decision on the spot. I would rather have that right hand cut off than to give an audience a week now to decide what to do with Jesus.[2]

I want to preach with that kind of urgency! We are not guaranteed a tomorrow. The people we preach to are not guaranteed to be back next week. We need to preach like our listeners are on fire and the only hope for putting the fire out is Christ. This is more than preaching Christ for the purpose of salvation. One of the most destructive things a preacher can do is tell people *what* to do without telling them *why*. This is what we do when we divorce the commands of God from the work of Christ. We are called to "preach Christ crucified" (1 Cor. 1:23). Nothing makes our preaching more distinctly Christian than preaching Christ. In fact, if you're not determined to preach Christ, the rest of us would ask you to quit because you're hurting our cause. A sermon without Christ is worthless, so preach Christ—and preach Him every week.

Manipulating People's Emotions

The relationship between preaching and emotions can be tricky. As is often the case, we tend to live in the extremes. Some preach in such a way as to intentionally avoid engaging listeners' emotions. Others seem to preach to people's emotions almost exclusively. In such cases, the sermon feels more like an infomercial than an exposition.

There is a thin line between appealing to listeners' emotions—which I've argued we should do in chapter 1—and trying to manipulate them. We should appeal to the whole person when we preach. We should appeal to the head by addressing the mind, the hands by applying the text to our lives, and the heart by appealing to the emotions. Good preaching should make us feel feelings, not just think thoughts. The news of our sin should break our hearts and cause us to mourn. The news of God's love should increase our affection for Him and gratitude toward Him. The news of Christ's finished work in our place and for our sin should make us want to give our whole lives to Him in response.

So what is the difference between appealing to people's emotions and trying to manipulate them? The biggest difference has to do with the motive of the preacher. When you start to utilize a formula meant to invoke the "right response" from people, you've crossed the line from appealing to manipulating. If you preach long enough, you'll start to realize that certain actions generate a certain response from people. The right song paired with the right story produces the "right response." This is dangerous territory. You are not trusting the Holy Spirit at this point. You are not relying on His power to use His Word to accomplish His plan in His people. Instead, you are manipulating people in order to control them or make yourself feel good by forcing some form of visible fruit. Both of these are a sorry substitute for the transforming power of the Holy Spirit. Appeal to people's emotions faithfully, but don't ever manipulate them.

Make any one of these three mistakes and you will most certainly crash and burn the close of your sermon. On the flip side, there a few ways to guarantee that you can close faithfully.

HOW TO LAND WELL

Close with Clarity

Clarity is king in communication. If you're not clear, people can't understand you. And again, you can't be faithful just to the text; you have to be faithful to your listeners as well. This means that it's not enough to be consistent with the text. You also have to be clear in the way you communicate it. This is true all the way to the closing moments of your sermon. It would be a shame to preach clearly all the way through only to close in such a way that causes people to think, *What is he trying to say?* We must strive for maximum clarity. Here are two specific principles regarding clarity that I strive to implement in my own conclusions.

Be clear about what Christ has done. Everything God calls us to *do* flows from the reality of what Christ has already *done*. As a result, we can never fail to be clear regarding Christ's finished work. My hope and prayer is that Christ permeates my entire sermon, but I especially want that to be true of the closing moments. God forbid people walk away with a long list of things to do divorced from the life-altering news of what

Christ has already done for them. That's the type of preaching that could be found in any mosque or temple. It creates moralists, not disciples of Jesus. If our sermons lack Christ, they lack the critical element that makes our preaching distinctly Christian. Furthermore, a sermon without Christ is dead before it starts. We preach Christ or we preach nothing.

My good friend Joe Thorn wrote an article on this topic titled "Killing Moralism."[3] In it he gives helpful insight on how to preach Christ effectively. Again, these principles should be incorporated throughout your sermon, but the conclusion serves as a great safety net on the off chance you've lacked clarity at any point along the way. First, he says we need to show the God of the command. God's commands are never detached from His character. Our job is to show that whatever we are called to as God's children flows from who He is.

Second, we need to show the grace behind the command. Everything God calls us to is for our good and made possible only by His grace. Joe writes,

> God does not reveal his will so that we can build our confidence in our ability to keep it, but so that we can exalt and exult in the God we know by grace. Showing the grace behind the command moves us from fearful performance-based religion to a delight in the will and ways of God.[4]

This is the only obedience that honors God.

Last, we must show the gospel above the command. Jesus has already paid the price for each of our failures. In addition, He lived a perfect life in our place, meaning He perfectly obeyed every command of God we fail to obey. Finally, His Spirit does in fact empower us to obey. If we are in Christ, we are no longer slaves to sin (Rom. 6:6–7). We're free to follow and obey. This is encouraging news for discouraged people.

Do not send God's people home without showing them the God of every command that you've called them to heed. Do not send them home without showing them God's grace in Christ behind those commands; always drive to the gospel above these commands. Only then have we been clear regarding what Christ has done. That said, God's Word still contains a multitude of commands we're called to obey, and we need to clearly convey them.

Be clear about what people are called to do. The finished work of Christ never negates the specific obedience He calls us to. The Bible is filled with imperatives we're called to obey. As you'll read in the next chapter, this is work we should do at every point in the sermon, but the conclusion in particular is a critical place to reinforce the application of the text. We never want people to walk away wondering what God's Word has just called them to do.

The close of your sermon is an appropriate point at which to drive people to the specific demands of the text. I want people headed home each Sunday still wrestling with their need to put into action what they've just heard in God's Word. Not wrestling because the message was unclear and they're not sure how to implement it, but wrestling because it was so clear that there is no way they cannot implement it. Let the text drive the specifics of the application, and let the Spirit drive the convicting and empowering work to follow it through.

Clarity is paramount in effective communication.

Commit to closing with clarity regarding what Christ has done and what God calls His people to do. If you are clear through the majority of your sermon but confusing as you close, it will cast a cloud over your entire sermon. Strive to close with maximum clarity.

Close Smoothly

Have you ever been on a flight with a bumpy landing? The kind where, for whatever reason, it feels like the plane touches down three, maybe four times as it finally bounces to a landing? It's disconcerting. Everyone grabs and squeezes the armrests as if the applied pressure will help the plane land more smoothly. Further, that bumpy landing usually proves to be the thing people remember most. The rest of the flight may be perfect, but when asked the obligatory, "How was your flight?" I can almost guarantee that the answer will be, "It was great, but the landing was bumpy." Likewise, if the close of your sermon is bumpy, people will primarily remember that. If the ending is smooth, they will remember what was strong about the sermon.

The quality of the close and the intentionality of our preparation are always connected. Again, I find the conclusion of the sermon to be one of the more difficult parts to write. I had a stretch longer than I'd care to admit where my conclusions consisted of a few scribbled lines at the end of my sermon that usually resulted in my bumping along, trying to find a place to land. I figured I could scratch out those few lines and "let the Spirit lead the rest" like I cautioned against at the outset of this chapter. This was and is laziness baptized in a sentiment that sounds spiritual. The Spirit leads just as much on Thursday in the study as He does Sunday on the stage. My problem was that I wasn't doing the necessary work of preparing my closing. Instead, I traded writing out a thoughtful conclusion for winging it.

Please—don't ever wing it. Even those who preach well with no notes (a practice I don't recommend) still labor over their preparation on the front end. A smooth close demands we take time to prepare both what we're going to close with and how we want to say it.

You first need to determine the specific content of your closing. Are you closing with a final insight or idea? Are you closing with a story meant to make a point? Are you simply reviewing where you've been? How will Christ be the hero of the sermon? Don't make this up on the spot. Don't trust yourself to "feel it out" in the moment. I've tried that; it almost never goes well. Instead, figure out the content, and then take the time to write it down.

Next you need to determine the specific tone of your closing. What you say is only half of the closing equation. How you say what you say has everything to do with the way it's received and how it makes people feel as a result. Will you conclude with an encouraging tone? Will you close with urgency by creating a crisis moment and calling people to a decision? Will your tone be confrontational? This is not to be glossed over. Choose carefully and thoughtfully so that people don't miss the content of your close because the tone was unhelpful.

While we need to strive for a clear and smooth closing, we have to labor over at least one more piece.

Close in a Timely Fashion

Some sermons are simply too long. Few preachers can preach for more than forty minutes without losing the attention of every listener in the room. Sadly, in certain tribes, lengthy sermons are often looked at with admiration. I've heard pastors brag about preaching for over an hour as if they expected a high five or some sort of spiritual chest bump.

Some say, "I'm just trying to say what the text says, and that takes time." I get that. But saying what the text says does not mean we have to say everything the text says in one sermon. You will get another opportunity to say all you need to say. And most listeners have a tough time sticking with a preacher for forty minutes, much less an hour.

I've gone over an hour before, and the only people more tired than I was after the fact were the people I'd punished by preaching so long. After preaching a few hundred sermons over the last ten years, I've discovered that thirty-seven to forty minutes is my sweet spot. Less than that and I feel rushed; more than that and I did not prepare well enough.

Charles Spurgeon knew a thing or two about preaching. His nickname was "The Prince of Preachers," after all. In his *Lectures to My Students*, Spurgeon included a chapter titled "Attention!" Here's what he says about sermon duration and losing listeners:

> In order to maintain attention, avoid being too long. An old preacher used to say to a young man who preached an hour, "My dear friend, I do not care what else you preach about, but I wish you would always preach about forty minutes." We ought seldom to go

much beyond that—forty minutes, or say, three-quarters of an hour. If a fellow cannot say all he has to say in that time, when will he say it?[5]

Of course, a sermon is more than a devotional. We're called to more than a mere sermonette each week. We should preach compelling and concise sermons every Sunday. If we work hard and prepare well, we can preach shorter sermons that pack a more powerful punch.

Endings matter. How many books have you read, movies have you seen, or TV series have you watched and loved that were ruined by a lousy ending? We don't want our otherwise strong sermons to be weakened by sloppy endings. Dig in and dedicate yourself to the preparation. Close clearly, smoothly, and in a timely fashion. You have an hour. Get at it.

6

FRIDAY
Fill in the Frame

---

*MILESTONE: To complete
preaching notes in two hours or less.*

If you've ever gone for a run, you've probably made the mistake of starting too fast. You feel good at the beginning, so you take off strong, but you quickly burn out because you can't sustain the pace you set. You can also err on the other end by running too slowly. Every competitive race ranging from a 5K to a marathon typically has a time by which contestants are supposed to finish. A sweeper car brings up the rear of the race, and if you fall too far behind, you will be disqualified and designated a nonfinisher.

Pacing is an issue not just in running, but also in preaching. Poor pacing is one of the biggest mistakes preachers make.

The best sermons explain the text, illustrate the text, and apply the text. The mistake we tend to make as preachers is spending too much or too little time on one of these three parts. For instance, if all you do is explain for forty minutes straight, you will wear your listeners out and lose them somewhere along the way. People need a break from the mental strain of striving to follow along. If you don't give them a break in the form of an illustration, they will take a break anyway by checking out. On the other hand, if you fly through your explanation of the text, using it to footnote rather than to ground everything you're preaching, your listeners will have a limited experience of God's work through His Word.

A skilled preacher must be strategic in his pacing. For me, this means carefully explaining, creatively illustrating, and prayerfully applying every point of my sermon. If you've followed this book's process thus far, your textual work is done, the frame is written, and you've already finished both your introduction and conclusion. This means all you have left is to fill in the frame. We want to take each point of the sermon we've framed and determine how to explain, illustrate, and apply it. This will help us best pace our sermon on Sunday. When I was a new preacher, I could understand what the biblical text said, but I was uncertain about what I was supposed to do with it. Knowing you need to explain, illustrate, and apply each point maps out exactly how you should proceed. You don't have to stare at a blank page while you wait for inspiration to strike. We know what we need, so let's talk about how to do it.

CAREFULLY EXPLAIN THE TEXT

Preacher, don't forget your call. We proclaim the Word of God (2 Tim. 4:2). Our primary task is not the propagation of our opinions, ideas, or creativity. We preach the Son of God from the Word of God to the glory of God, or we're not preaching. This means we start with the text itself. We want to focus attention on what it actually says. In order to do so, we need to explain various features of or relating to the text.

Explain Words

The Holy Spirit inspired not only the ideas of Scripture, but also the words of Scripture (2 Tim. 3:16; 2 Peter 1:20–21). That means both the words and ideas of Scripture matter. This is why I choose to preach from a more literal English translation. If the Holy Spirit inspired the original author to use a specific word, we should strive to translate it as closely as possible. This also means we need to help our congregations grapple with the words themselves. We need to explain words that have unclear meanings. We should draw out nuances from the original languages that may not come through clearly in our English translations. We should not let people import their own meaning onto the words or conveniently skip over words they wish were not there. Words have meaning, and it is our job to draw them out. Explaining the text means explaining the words of the text.

Explain History

Each text has a historical context that often informs or influences the way we should interpret and understand any given section of Scripture. As I write this chapter, I'm preaching through the book of Jonah in my own church. One of the points I've tried to make clear is that there was a specific segment of history in which the story took place. Understanding that era helps us better understand why Jonah felt such strong disdain for the city of Nineveh and its inhabitants. An important part of explaining the text is providing any significant historical and cultural details that help us better comprehend the meaning of what God is saying to us. Be a student of history. Study good commentary. Do your best to understand what is happening both in and around the text you are preaching. Explaining the text means explaining history.

Explain Significance

Sometimes we gloss over words without understanding their significance. We have to stop and ask ourselves, *Why does this warning, promise, command, or word matter?* For instance, I remember the first time a Bible teacher drew my attention to the importance of noting words like *therefore* in Scripture. As a preacher, if I drop into a text that starts with the word *therefore*, it's important for me to recognize there is a prior principle or declaration present in the passage that I must help listeners understand before I drive home the implications of the current passage. For example, when Jesus says, "Go therefore and make disciples of all nations" in Matthew 28:19, that "therefore" drives us back to verse 18, where Jesus says, "All authority in heaven and on earth has been given to me." The Great Commission flows out of the infinite authority of Jesus. It's our responsibility to explain the significance of every warning, command, and promise of Scripture. Explaining the text means explaining significance.

Explain Details

This is especially important when preaching a narrative text. Preaching narrative is all about putting people in the story. We want to draw from the details themselves the setting, the scene, and the scenery surrounding the story we are preaching. We want people to be able to envision the Sea of Galilee, to feel the isolation of being a leper, to grasp the gruesome nature of crucifixion and all it meant for Jesus. We want them to imagine being with the disciples and feeling their fear when they saw Jesus walking on the water, to consider what it would have been like to see Lazarus walk out of that tomb, to experience the joy and confusion of seeing Jesus in the flesh after watching Him die. This demands that we delve deeply into the details and that we take people with us. We don't need to fabricate details. They are often provided in the text. We just have to explain them.

I'm sure you could add to this list. I hope my list simply gets you thinking about all that needs explaining. What matters is that we take the time to describe everything critical to comprehending what God intends for us in each point. We can never become so familiar with the Bible that we cease being blown away by what it says. Explaining the text means embracing the details.

CREATIVELY ILLUSTRATE THE TEXT

When we explain the text, we're answering the question, "What does it say?" When we illustrate the text, we're answering the question, "What does it mean?" If all you do is explain what the text says, you're not a preacher, but a commentator.

We have to tell people what every verse of Scripture actually means. This is why we labor to creatively illustrate every point of every text. A good illustration is important for at least three reasons: it helps people further grasp the meaning, it allows them to catch their breath mentally, and it draws back those who might have wandered off mentally.

An illustration can be anything from a personal story that sheds light on what you're saying to a current-day example of something that clarifies a point in Scripture that is unclear to modern audiences due to cultural differences between us and those to whom the text was originally written. You can also use a compelling story from history, the news, media, literature—you name it. The problem is that good illustrations can be difficult to find and require practice to use them well. Here are a few precautions to help you keep a weak illustration from ruining your sermon.

Never Be the Hero of Your Own Illustration

I remember going to a pastors' conference years ago and listening to a pastor preach on making disciples in the local church. Over and again he would give a principle for maximizing missional living, explain how most churches and Christians fail to apply this principle, and then use himself as an illustration of how to do it right. I don't believe this pastor was arrogant or proud, but hearing him herald himself as the hero of his principles was off-putting nonetheless. Nobody wants to hear about your superiority at every point of your own sermon. And by the way, you're not superior at every point of your sermon, and neither am I. As a general rule, if you're going to use a personal story as an illustration, err on the side of being self-deprecating. Humbly and appropriately use yourself as an example of what not to do rather than run the risk of being the hero and appearing arrogant.

Be Certain of What You're Trying to Say

The riskiest part of every sermon is always the illustration. It either clarifies or confuses. There is no middle ground. When I first started preaching, I didn't write out my illustrations. Instead, I would simply write a word or a phrase as a mental trigger and then tell the story or principle that was attached to that illustration. I ended this practice after an embarrassing crash and burn with a bad illustration. It involved a story about Jean-Claude Van Damme. Yep, *the* Jean-Claude Van Damme, martial arts film star. I remember reading a story about how he was beaten up by a bouncer in a bar fight and thinking how ironic that was based on the action icon he was at the time. The problem was—aside from the fact that I was using Van Damme as an illustration in the first place—in the middle of my illustration, I realized I had no idea where I was going, and I could tell by the confused looks on the faces of the few people listening that neither did anyone else. To this day, I call an illustration that gets away from me "Van Damming." It was horrible.

To ensure an illustration truly clarifies and doesn't muddle the meaning of the text, I craft a clear sentence at the top and bottom of the written narrative of the illustration that sums up the idea I'm going to illustrate. This anchors the illustration and ensures it won't derail. Beware of "off-the-cuff" illustrations. To avoid "Van Damming," always be certain of what you're trying to say.

Be Careful with Pop-Culture Illustrations

Referring to television, music, and movies always runs at least four risks. First, it might distract from what is important. The last thing you want to happen when you make a reference to *The Lord of the Rings*, *Star Wars*, or *The Chronicles of Narnia*—I'm a nerd, so these would be my go-tos—is to see everyone's eyes glaze over because they've started thinking about how much they want your sermon to end so they can go home and watch the movie you've referenced. What you intended as a help instantly became a hindrance.

Second, a pop-culture reference may alienate your listeners. Have you ever experienced that awkward moment when you ask something like, "How many of you saw *Dancing with the Stars* last night?" and only three people raise their hand? It's brutal. It means the illustration you thought was going to perfectly land your point will make sense only to the three people who saw the show. It alienates everyone else and leaves them foggy as to what you're trying to communicate.

Third, an illustration from pop culture might devalue your point. When we seek to illustrate subject matter like the atonement, divine sovereignty, or grace with references to reality TV, sitcoms, or movies, we run the risk of making these breathtaking and beautiful themes in Scripture appear cheap and trivial. We must always do the hard work of seeking out appropriate illustrations for the truths we are expounding.

Finally, you always run the risk of offending someone when you reference pop culture. Everyone has differing convictions concerning media intake. What serves as entertainment for one person often offends another. An innocent reference to a song, band, show, or movie can instantly and unintentionally offend someone, destroy your credibility, and rob you of the opportunity for input into their life.

Don't get me wrong. I'm not suggesting we never use pop culture as fodder for illustrations. I'm simply saying we should always evaluate the risk of using such illustrations and determine whether using them is worth the risk. You may find that a movie reference is the perfect way to make your point, or you may discover that laziness has left you looking for the cheapest, easiest illustration you can think of. Let's prayerfully, patiently, and diligently seek out the best ways to illustrate the great message God has given us to proclaim.

Don't Get Stuck in a Rut

Occasionally, I find myself using the same type of illustration week after week. I'll realize that I've used stories about my kids for a month straight or referred to exercise as an example so many times that it sounds like I spend more time in the gym than I do at my job. This is a problem. It's not that the illustrations aren't accurate but that they become less effective. This is one reason to try living an interesting life. Read widely. Try new things. Get a hobby. Go on adventures. Everything you do has the opportunity to help you illustrate better. If all you do is work and watch Netflix, the well from which you draw sermon illustrations will run dry or leave you in a rut.

Ask Others for Help

Developing illustrations can be the most elusive aspect of sermon preparation for many pastors. One reason they are difficult for me is that I have to come up with an average of five to seven each week. I've stopped coming up with all the illustrations I need on my own. I now have several people I go to for help. I simply explain what I'm trying to illustrate, typically by reading them the specific line I anticipate using to transition to my illustration, and then ask them something like, "What comes to mind when you hear this?" More often than not, they either have a great idea or they say something that sparks an idea in my mind. Drawing others into the process takes much of the pressure off me and helps me avoid falling into an illustration rut.

Illustrations are important to get right. I've found that people remember the illustrations I've used far more than any principle or carefully crafted sentence I've conveyed. Illustrations are a tool we need to wield wisely.

PRAYERFULLY APPLY THE TEXT

Few things put more dread in my heart than pulling into an IKEA parking lot. We're talking nausea, cold sweats, and fervent-prayer-for-the-second-coming-of-Christ kind of dread. If you've never had the "pleasure" of exploring the Swedish megastore, it's truly a thing to behold. Imagine the crowds of an amusement park, the stress of a Walmart on Black Friday, and the pain of a root canal all rolled into one. It's basically the worst place on earth to me. The real kicker about IKEA is that you have to assemble everything you purchase, which actually does feel like rocket science. Walking around the store and finding a piece of furniture you want to take home is easier than actually putting it together. I always head home with a clear picture in my head of *what* I want to build. It's the *how* of building it that I struggle with. Without the instructions, I'd have no hope of moving from what I want to do to actually doing it.

When it comes to applying God's Word, it is one thing to have a general idea of *what* you're supposed to do and another to know *how* to do it. James 1:22–25 is an essential and necessary warning about the importance of applying the truth of God's Word:

> But be doers of the word, and not hearers only, deceiving yourselves. For if anyone is a hearer of the word and not a doer, he is like a man who looks intently at his natural face in a mirror. For he looks at himself and goes away and at once forgets what he was like. But the one who looks into the perfect law, the law of liberty, and perseveres, being no hearer who forgets but a doer who acts, he will be blessed in his doing.

The scenario described here is borderline absurd, and that's the idea. It's inconceivable that the average person would look at their face in a mirror and then walk away, forgetting what their own face looks like. In the same way, it should be inconceivable for a Christian to hear something in Scripture and then fail to apply it. In John 14:15, Jesus said, "If you love me, you will keep my commandments." And this is verse 23: "If anyone loves me, he will keep my word." Disciples of Jesus are doers of the Word. We act on and apply all that we acquire from the Word of God. As preachers, we have a responsibility for more than telling people what they're supposed to do. We also have to teach them how to do it.

We've already explained what the text says and illustrated

what it means, but we haven't finished the task until we've unpacked what it means *for us*. The final question to be asked is, "What implications does this text hold in our lives?" Faithful preaching answers this question by taking listeners by the hand and helping them know how to apply these principles in their lives. Bryan Chapell writes,

> Application fulfills the obligations of exposition. . . . Without application, a preacher has no reason to preach, because truth without actual or potential application fulfills no redemptive purpose. This means that at its heart, preaching is not merely the proclamation of the truth but truth applied.[1]

Learning to do the work of "truth applied" takes time, effort, and usually trial and error. Here are a few simple points to keep in mind.

Unpack the "What"

Has someone ever given you driving directions that were so convoluted that you were more confused afterward than you were before? "You take Third Street up to Fifth and then turn left. You take that to Fifteenth Avenue, drive northwest, and go right until you get to where the McDonalds used to be. You do a U-turn and come back down Radiator Boulevard until you get up to eighty-eight miles per hour and your flux capacitor kicks in, taking you back to 1985. Then you'll see my house. It's red. You got all that?" You're like, "Huh?" Such experiences are disorienting and common to us all.

Clarity is key to application. People need to understand

what exactly they're supposed to do. Is there an attitude to abandon? Is there specific rebellion to repent of? Is there a prescribed or implied action we need to take? The clearer we can be, the more likely it is that people will comply. Apart from our help, listeners are, at best, left to assume or guess at what the text is calling them to do. At worst, and probably most frequently, no action is taken, because there is no clear application coming from the pulpit. If we're going to help people be doers of the Word, we have to unpack what exactly they're called to do.

Unpack the "Why"

God is after more than behavior that conforms to His Word. He is also after transformed hearts. I recently asked my son to take a pair of his socks up to his room. He had done his typical "disrobing" the moment he had walked into the house from school and had thrown them on the floor. After a moment of whining about how unrealistic my expectations were, he grabbed the socks, stomped across the house, and marched up the stairs to his room, where he put them into the laundry hamper. He then stomped back down the stairs and back to what he had been doing before. My heart didn't exactly swell with pride during this moment. Sure, my son had done what I asked, but he hadn't done it with a great attitude. Agreed? I don't want my kids to simply obey; I also want them to *want* to obey. God is the same way.

Psalm 1:2 says that blessed is the man whose "delight is in the law of the LORD." That has several meanings, but at least one implication is that we should love God's Word and desire to obey it. One of our many jobs as preachers, then, is to help people understand why they should conform their hearts, minds, and lives to the specific application Scripture calls them to. When we omit the "why," we detach action from attitude and concoct a recipe for making legalists and Pharisees, not lovers of Jesus who obey joyfully. God is after so much more than mere obedience. He's after our hearts. To win the heart, we have to unpack why the specific application is so important.

Unpack the "How"

I think of this as giving people "handles" to grab. We recently spent a day as a family at a rock-climbing gym to celebrate Tami's birthday. None of us are experienced climbers, but it was tons of fun, even though my hands were ripped up and bloodied by the end of the day. Now, the "what" of climbing is pretty simple, right? You start at the bottom, and your objective is to get to the top. That's pretty much it. But just because the objective is simple doesn't mean the process is. The challenge is to make sure you find the right handles within your reach in order to get to the top. That's the way I think about the "how" of application.

As preachers, we need to give people the necessary handles to help them reach the specific application God is after. When Paul says, "Husbands, love your wives, as Christ loved the church and gave himself up for her" (Eph. 5:25), the objective—the "what"—is clear: love your wives. You don't need to be able to read Greek to figure that out. What men will most likely still need help with, however, is the "how." Paul says we're to love our wives the way Christ loved the church. So what does that mean for us? Well, Christ loved the church by giving Himself up, by sacrificing Himself for our good. If I were going to unpack the "how" of this verse, I'd spend time wrestling with what sacrificing myself for my wife would look like. These are handles, specific "hows," that help us accomplish whatever the text has called us to. Once you've thought through these three parts—the "what," the "why," and the "how"—write them in your sermon notes. Don't leave this work to your listeners. Our job is to be helpful by leading them to obedience.

The work of explaining, illustrating, and applying the text is difficult. Friday tends to be the most draining day of preparation for me, even when I have worked the process and have stuck to my daily milestones. If this is true for you, too, don't lose heart. Pacing your sermon effectively is critical, and laboring for these three parts at each point will help you achieve good pacing. You're almost there. You've worked hard and have a few hours to go. Plant yourself at the desk, dig deep, and fill in that frame.

7

SUNDAY
Finish Strong

MILESTONE: To prime your heart and mind, pray for your preaching, and prepare your notes in one hour.

Every Sunday morning, I wake up with a strange mix of excitement and nerves. All the struggle of preparing is behind me, and I'm just hours away from pouring out everything I've wrestled with all week. I usually feel a brief sense of panic in that place between being half asleep and half awake as I can't, for a moment, remember anything from my sermon. I actually used to have a recurring nightmare on Saturday nights that involved me stepping into the pulpit, looking down at my notes, and finding nothing prepared. As every eye looked on, I would start to mumble and make up a sermon out of thin air. I'd love to report that the dreams end with me preaching an earth-rattling, hell-shattering sermon resulting in revival, but more often than not, I wake up just before falling off a stage I never should have set foot on.

After this brief panic subsides, the anticipation sets in. It feels like game day. Sports consumed most of my younger years. Football, baseball, track, basketball—if you could compete in it, I wanted to participate in it. Similar to sermon prep, I never loved preparation in sports, but game day was always my favorite day of the week. It was finally time to put all the practice to work. Every game day I followed similar rituals. I listened to the same music, ate the same meals, and walked through the same stretches and warm-ups. It helped me calm my nerves and focus my attention on the task in front of me.

I approach Sunday morning the same way. I tend to stick to the same rituals week after week, because having a consistent routine helps me better prepare my heart and mind to preach. I want to commend the same practice to you. You are not done preparing your sermon until after it has been preached. Sunday is not the day to sleep in and coast to the finish line. There is still critical work to do. These final hours prior to preaching can make or break your sermon. While you will need to develop your own routines and rituals, here are three essential rituals for Sunday morning that I believe can work for all preachers.

PRIME YOUR HEART AND MIND

I have a theory about Sunday morning and spiritual warfare for preachers. Based on the last fifteen years of my life as a pastor and preacher (which I realize may seem like nothing compared to the years others have put in), I believe preachers are often hit hardest by spiritual attacks on Sunday mornings. The early hours of Sunday morning can be disproportionately dark, discouraging, and even depressing for me. I often feel more overwhelmed on Sunday mornings than any other time of the week. All of this occurs just prior to stepping up to preach, which I believe is the most important thing I do all week.

The attack of the enemy is always greatest when the threat to his kingdom is most imminent. Every sermon is a declaration of war on this world and the one who seeks to rule it. Paul calls Satan "the god of this world" (2 Cor. 4:4). John tells us "the whole world lies in the power of the evil one" (1 John 5:19). Every sermon is spiritual warfare. That warfare starts in the study and moves into the sanctuary. The intensity of the attack you experience increases the urgency of your need to combat it. When attacked, we don't lie down in defeat. Instead, we stand in the victory Christ has already won, and we fight back.

Fighting back against the ever-present Sunday-morning spiritual attack starts with priming my heart and mind. To prime something is to prepare it for action or use. The idiom "priming the pump" originated in the late 1800s in reference to the process of pouring liquid into a pump to expel the air and prepare it for work. Priming is a regular process in our lives. I prime my coffee cup in the morning by filling it with hot water prior to pouring coffee into it. I prime my mind for the day by drinking said coffee and by taking a hot shower. I prime my body for strength training by jogging. Priming something prepares it for action or use.

No part of me needs priming more on Sunday morning than my heart and mind. And nothing primes my heart for action like ascribing worth to the One I'm called to proclaim boldly. When I drive to my study on Sunday mornings, I lift my voice in worship through song. Music has an amazing amount of influence on the heart and mind. It informs the way we think and feel. It can lift a lousy mood and encourage a despairing heart. We're blessed to live in a culture where nearly all music is easily accessible, and there has never been such an abundance of God-centered, Jesus-exalting, Spirit-filled, and biblically saturated songs to sing. It's even easy to find whatever type of worship genre you prefer. Traditional, contemporary, folk, and gospel worship are all just a click away. Let's not waste this great gift. Pick your preferred style, turn it up loud, and lift your voice to God.

The louder I sing, the quieter my doubts get. The more I look at the greatness of God, the smaller my problems become. The longer I look at the cross, the less shame due to my sin hangs over my head. This demands intentionality. We don't just wake up with hearts and minds ready to preach. They need to be primed. Worship is one powerful way to do this.

A second source God uses to prime my heart and mind to preach is His Word. As much as possible, I try not to skip my devotions on Sunday morning. I never want to simply rely on what God has spoken to me throughout the past week. I need to go to the well of God's Word for a fresh drink daily—and especially before preaching. I tend to have a reading plan I'm working through in addition to my daily sermon preparation. I just stick to my plan, and without fail God in His providence has something timely for me wherever I'm at in Scripture that day.

Every Sunday when I open the Scriptures, I'm reminded that God is good, great, gracious, and glorious. I am convicted of my sin and am called to my Savior. I'm comforted by the promises of all God has done, is doing, and has yet to do. More than anything, my heart and mind are recalibrated to the power and prominence of the God I'm about to proclaim.

This priming warms my heart and sharpens my mind. It prepares me for the privilege of preaching that God has given me to accomplish. If your habit has been simply to review your notes or to sleep in with barely enough time to make it to church, I'd commend this practice to you. Give yourself some extra space, and prioritize the priming of your heart and mind before you proceed into these final stages of preparation.

PRAY OVER YOUR PREACHING

Prayer is a natural progression from the priming we just discussed. Any preacher would be foolish to preach a single word without first petitioning God to do what only He can do. While I never set out to make a recurring prayer list for Sunday morning, here are a few requests I pray regularly.

God, guard my speech. I have a tongue that tends to run quicker than my mind, and I communicate for a living. This is a dangerous combination. A quick tongue and a faulty filter go together like fire and gasoline. Some of my greatest regrets are times when I've said something "off the cuff" in the pulpit that was questionable. It may be an unplanned comment, a phrase that lacks clarity and causes confusion, or even something that may in some way lack godliness. I've prayed the heart of Ephesians 4:29 more times than I can count: "Let no corrupting talk come out of your mouths, but only such as is good for building up, as fits the occasion, that it may give grace to those who hear." That's what I'm after. But to be honest, I have so much room to grow here. I need God to sanctify every part of me, including my speech. God forbid we ever speak even one word that is biblically inaccurate or pastorally insensitive. I need help in this area, so every Sunday, without fail, I ask God to guard my speech.

God, soak my heart in the sermon I've prepared. I never want my sermon to sound like I'm trying recite lines I've written. Some preachers are so ill prepared or overly concerned with rhetorical precision that they end up sounding like a prepubescent boy trying to remember lines in his first junior-high play. It's awkward, unnatural, and distracting. I want to prepare every word yet preach in such a way that it flows naturally, spilling from the overflow of my heart. This is why I ask God to soak my heart in the sermon. Each week, I ask Him to press the notes I've prepared deep into my heart and mind so I can remember what I've prepared. I don't want to be buried in my notes when I'm preaching to people.

The first step is to get the sermon *on the page.* You may not write a word-for-word manuscript—though I do commend this to new preachers—but you should write out the vast majority of what you plan to say. Roughly 90 percent of my sermon is written on the page. The second step is to get the sermon *in my heart* so I can then preach it to others. Like everything else, I need the Lord's help in this. Like a needy child, I ask my loving Father for help in this intensely practical and absolutely important aspect of my preaching.

God, protect my tone. One of my great fears is saying the right thing the wrong way. I've heard my friend James Mac-Donald say, "If you're wrong in the way that you're right, you're wrong even if you're right." This has major implications when it comes to tone in preaching. *How* you say what you say is as important as *what* you say. As I've said, it's critical that our tone mirrors the text. Saying what God says but missing the heart from which He says it is as damaging as misrepresenting what God has said. For instance, the New Testament contains many hard sayings of Jesus, but He is not harsh. In Matthew 11:29, Jesus says, "Take my yoke upon you, and learn from me, for I am *gentle*" (emphasis added). If we repeat a hard saying that Jesus said and say it harshly, we are misrepresenting His heart and character. Furthermore, if we are cold in the way we address sin or call people to repentance, we misrepresent the compassionate heart of God. Psalm 78:38 says, "Yet [God], being *compassionate*, atoned for their iniquity and did not destroy them; he restrained his anger often and did not stir up all his wrath" (emphasis added). Faithfulness to the text is a non-negotiable for Bible preachers, and faithfulness to the text demands that we be faithful in our tone. To do this, we need God's help, so we ask Him to protect our tone.

God, prepare the hearts of those listening. The parable of the sower in Matthew 13 has to be one of the most humbling stories for preachers. It highlights that not everyone will be receptive to the word of the gospel when preached. No matter what you say or how you say it, some will respond and some will not. Paul reminds us that "neither he who plants nor he who waters is anything, but only God who gives the growth" (1 Cor. 3:7). And in John 6:44, Jesus says, "No one can come to me unless the Father who sent me draws him." People's receptivity to the gospel rests in the hands of God, not in the hands of preachers. This alone should drive us to our knees quickly and constantly. You can preach like a man on fire, and people may even clap and affirm your passion with an obligatory "Amen." But no one other than the Spirit of God can open a heart to receive His Word. That's why every Sunday I ask God to prepare people's hearts in whatever way is necessary for them to welcome what God says and to leave changed.

God, grant me unction. The word *unction* simply means "anointing." The Puritans and Reformers understood unction to be the type of powerful and passionate preaching enabled by the Holy Spirit. As preachers, we are desperate for the Holy Spirit to rest on and work in and through us as we preach. Unction—the Spirit of God using the Word of God—makes preaching pierce the hearts of those listening. Unction is not about being inspirational or loud, and it's far more than mere excitement about the topic or text being preached. Unction doesn't comes from inside us. It comes only from God and thus demands that we beg Him for it. Charles Spurgeon put it this way:

> One bright benison which private prayer brings down upon the ministry is an indescribable and inimitable something, better understood than named; it is a dew from the Lord, a divine presence which you will recognize at once when I say it is "an unction from the Holy One." What is it? I wonder how long we might beat our brains before we could plainly put into words what is meant by preaching with unction; yet he who preaches knows its presence, and he who hears soon detects its absence.[1]

I want this. Per Spurgeon's point, unction may be difficult to define, but I know I want it. I want the Spirit of God to work through my preaching, because if He does not, what's the point of preaching?

I can't overstress the fact that this "unction" is from God and comes to us through prayer. Methodist minister and Civil War chaplain E. M. Bounds wrote,

> This unction comes to the preacher not in the study but in the closet. It is heaven's distillation in answer to prayer. It is the sweetest exhalation of the Holy Spirit. It impregnates, suffuses, softens, percolates, cuts and soothes. It carries the Word like dynamite, like salt, like sugar; makes the Word a soother, an arranger, a revealer, a searcher; makes the hearer a culprit or a saint, makes him weep like a child and live like a giant; opens his heart and his purse as gently, yet as strongly as the spring opens the leaves. This unction is not the gift of genius. It is not found in the halls of learning. No eloquence can woo it. No industry can win it. No prelatical hands can confer it. It is the gift of God— the signet set to his own messengers. It is heaven's knighthood given to the chosen true and brave ones who have sought this anointed honor through many an hour of tearful, wrestling prayer.[2]

The only true power a preacher has is that of the One preached. We need His help, His power, His unction. So let's storm the throne of God and humbly ask Him to supply it.

PREPARE YOUR NOTES

Now that we have primed our hearts and minds and have prayed over our preaching, all that's left is the final preparation of our preaching notes. I know some prefer to preach from no notes, a practice I will address in appendix 1. For now, I simply want to say that I believe it is unwise for most preachers to attempt any sermon without the use of notes. I know that some do it effectively, but they are exceptions and should not be emulated by the rest of us. The vast majority of preachers will take at least an outline or some form of a manuscript into the pulpit, and it's critical that we prepare our notes before we preach.

By this point your notes are written, and you should be about 90 percent done. Hopefully at the eleventh hour on Sunday morning you're not still writing, reading commentary, or figuring out what you're going to say. If you are, go back to chapters 2 and 6. Working from the assumption, however, that by Sunday morning your preaching notes are finished, there is still one critical step that I find essential: vandalizing my notes in order to internalize them.

In terms of presentation, I'm not sure anything is worse than reading a manuscript word for word. No one wants to hear you read. You can't just write a good sermon. You have to *preach* it. This means you have to get the sermon inside of you so that it can come out of you in a clear, convicting, and compelling manner. This is why I "vandalize" my notes.

After I've printed out my typed notes, I edit, circle, and underline key words, sentences, and phrases that I want to jump off the page at me. I write out missing transitions, jot down a few final illustrations if needed, and maybe write clarifications regarding the implications of the text. I want to ensure the sermon is complete. I don't want to leave any listeners behind because I made assumptions or jumped from one point to another without making the cognitive connections necessary for people to follow me.

I have attempted to write out my entire sermon by hand, but that has never worked well for me. What has proven helpful is writing over the typed notes I take into the pulpit. This ritual helps engrain on my heart and mind what I've written.

I also highlight my notes in various colors so they can serve as visual triggers. I want to be certain that I can quickly identify where I am at and need to be when I glance at my notes. A terrifying experience I had as a teenager has given me an ironclad commitment to this practice. I still break out in a cold sweat when I think about the first time I was forced to speak publicly in high school. If I recall correctly, I gave a biographical speech on the great Notre Dame football coach Knute Rockne. I had written out my notes on 3 x 5 notecards as instructed by my teacher. When my name was called to give my speech, I nervously stepped up to the podium at the front of the classroom and launched into my introduction. Unfortunately, as I looked down at my cards, I might as well have been blind, because I lost my place in the sea of black and white. I started to panic, believing I would never find my place, would now have no friends, would probably never graduate high school, and would thus have to live at home while continuing to clean cabins at the local campground for the rest of my life. That may sound like an overreaction, but all those things went through my mind in a single moment. If only I had marked up my cards!

I learned this practice from Pastor James MacDonald, who has taught me more about preaching than any other person. I have taken much of what he does and have made it my own. I highlight all my main points or anything that will be on the screen in blue. Illustrations are in green. Textual comments are in yellow, while all my points of application are marked in pink. Lastly, I highlight all my word-for-word transitions in orange.

Sometimes people will catch a glimpse of my notes and think I've lost my mind. "How in the world do you preach from that?" they ask. It's a fair question, because when I'm done, my notes are quite the creative and colorful mess. But somehow this is how I get them in me, and I believe that if you vandalize your own notes, you, too, will better internalize them.

Generally, this all takes me about an hour on Sunday morning. When I skip any one of these rituals, I feel off. I know that these final steps are an important part of my preparation, so to ignore any one of them would cut a critical corner resulting in a sermon that has not been given my full effort. Your routines may look different than mine. You may prime your heart and mind in a way that I don't. The specifics of what you pray prior to preaching on Sunday morning may be different than mine. How you prepare the notes you preach from and what they look like will certainly reflect your preferences. My hope is not that you will conform to the specifics of my rituals. I've shared them by way of example and to help you think through your own. I do, however, hope you will be mindful of the principles driving your routines. If you do not view Sunday morning as part of your sermon-prep process, you are missing out on an important opportunity to maximize your preparation.

All the blood, sweat, and tears shed this week are about to culminate in a sermon God will use to impact those listening. Don't cut any corners now. Lift your voice, open the Bible, get on your knees, and break out the highlighters. It's almost game time, so get to work.

CONCLUSION
Work the Process

I'm writing this final chapter on a Sunday night. I'm worn out the way I am every Sunday night. I preached wholeheartedly yet again this morning. The sermon wasn't perfect, but it was the best I could do. I'm recounting my mistakes, hoping to learn and grow from them. But I'm also aware that I need to turn the page and not dwell on them. I wish I would have said some things differently or more clearly. I got tongue-tied at one point trying to get just one word out, which is always humbling as you watch people straining to guess the word you can't seem to spit out. I had to follow my notes a little too closely at several points and wish I'd had my thoughts better imprinted upon my heart and mind. Like most weeks, it wasn't my best sermon, but it certainly wasn't my worst. But most importantly, I left it all in the pulpit.

My voice is tired and so is my mind. I poured myself out, and now I'm left to pray that the Holy Spirit will seal away the work He started in hearts this morning. Tonight I'll lay down confident in the promise that God's Word never returns void (Isa. 55:11). I can't guarantee that every life was changed, but I can rest knowing that God's Spirit used His Word in every way He wanted to. I will sleep well tonight.

Accompanying the peace that comes from knowing that

God used His Word in the hearts and lives of many this morning is the overwhelming reality that I have to do it all over again this week. While one week of preparation and preaching comes to an end, another starts tomorrow. A fresh text. Another sermon to frame. More illustrations to find. New application to wrestle with. It would be overwhelming if I didn't love preaching so much. As this week ends and another begins, I'm left to think about the week ahead and the sermon I have to write. We have covered an immense amount of ground throughout these pages, and I want to leave you with a few closing encouragements in no particular order.

COMMIT YOURSELF TO PRAYER

This nail deserves to be driven one last time due to its impact and our ability to neglect it. One thing I find difficult about prayer is that it feels passive. I know we don't like to admit sentiments like this as pastors, but it's true. Cognitively, I know there is nothing more powerful and pointed than petitioning God for the help necessary to write and preach faithful sermons week in and week out. But I often feel that harder work, deeper study, and better processes are the secret sauce of sermon prep. All these matter, of course. The problem is that I tend to cling to these more naturally than I do to prayer. Concerning the importance of prayer in the life of the preacher, E. M. Bounds writes,

> Prayer is not a little habit pinned on to us while we were tied to our mother's apron strings; neither is it a little decent quarter of a minute's grace said over

an hour's dinner, but it is a most serious work of our most serious years. It engages more of time and appetite than our longest dinings or richest feasts. The prayer that makes much of our preaching must be made much of. The character of our praying will determine the character of our preaching. Light prayer will make light preaching. Prayer makes preaching strong, gives it unction, and makes it stick. In every ministry [that is] weighty for good, prayer has always been a serious business.[1]

Despite my deficiency in the practice of prayer, I could not agree with this more. I need this reminder, and my guess is that you do as well. Prayer and sermon preparation should not be separated. They're like peanut butter and jelly, spaghetti and meatballs, R2-D2 and C-3PO. They belong together. Whatever you do this week, make sure prayer is at the heart of it.

PRIORITIZE YOUR PREPARATION

Every week has its fair share of matters that feel urgent. A critical component of leadership is learning to discern the difference between things that feel urgent and things that actually are urgent. Furthermore, pastors have to develop the courage necessary to define the difference for themselves rather than allow others define it for them. Everyone has issues that feel urgent to them. But you can't allow every perceived emergency to become yours. I'd humbly submit to you that faithful pastors and effective preachers must prioritize sermon preparation over nearly everything else. True emergencies do happen.

People pass away unexpectedly. Relationships demand attention. Sometimes fires break out—literally.

When the church I helped to plant was just over a year old, a massive electrical fire broke out midweek in the theater we rented and incinerated the entire lobby. We were then notified that we would not be able to use the facility that weekend. We had just a few days to find a space to gather that coming Sunday. This was a true emergency. It was an urgent issue that demanded much of my attention that week. Burying my head in a book for hours on end would have done no good if we'd had no place to worship that weekend. We had to find another venue, and while I did have a sermon ready for Sunday, much of my time was preoccupied with this other problem. Emergencies indeed happen, but they are rarer than we'd like to admit.

Most of what gets in the way of diligent sermon preparation is our own inability to discipline ourselves. So many other things attract our focus. But when we neglect preparation—a priority indeed—the sermon inevitably suffers, and so will the church.

SCHEDULE YOUR BLOCKS

I assume you use a calendar to manage your week. If you don't, get one. I use the calendar app on my phone. Without it, I'd never be where I'm supposed to be or do the things I'm supposed to do. Maybe you hate technology and don't want to use an app. That's fine. I don't care if you use a Trapper Keeper with a print calendar so long as you have a way to schedule the time necessary for the critical task of sermon prep. We've set daily milestones with determined deadlines in different chapters throughout this book. Load these directly into your calendar, and then stick to what you've scheduled. It's simple, but it's not easy. It takes discipline, but it's worth it.

ELIMINATE DISTRACTIONS

We live in the most distracted culture ever. We have so many things vying for our attention at any given moment that it's a miracle we get anything done. We've already discussed that seemingly urgent issues attempt to pull our attention away from sermon prep. In addition to that, we have both the blessing and the curse of Twitter, Facebook, Instagram, Snapchat, YouTube, and whatever other app some twenty-year-old genius in a hoodie develops between my writing this book and your reading it. Social media, emails, books, people—these constantly seek our attention.

Attention is one of the great battlefields of our day, and as a pastor you have to fight to give your attention to what matters most. In order for you and me to write faithful sermons in the few hours we've allotted, we have to bring maximum focus that is free of all distraction to our prep time. Your context will determine what this looks like for you. I hang a Do Not Disturb sign on my study door when I am preparing. I turn off my email, put my phone away, stay off social media, and wear noise-canceling headphones. I rarely do sermon prep in public spaces anymore. We have to be able to sustain deep concentration for these hours in order to maximize them.[2] Take whatever measures necessary to eliminate any distractions that may detract from your ability to focus during these blocks.

SET A TIMER

Remember, one of the irreplaceable principles we've discussed is working with determined deadlines. I believe self-imposed constraints promote creativity and productivity. Deadlines have a way of sharpening our focus and driving us to accomplish what we need to. For instance, I'd bet my 2002 Ford Explorer—including the sweet tape deck in the dashboard console—that if I took you to a track and told you to run a lap as fast as you could, that you'd run hard and probably turn in a decent time. But if I told you that you had two minutes to run the same lap, my guess is that your time would be considerably faster, even if you couldn't finish under two minutes. Deadlines focus our attention and drive us harder.

The same is true for sermon prep. If I have an entire day to accomplish what I need to, I never get as much accomplished as when I have clear constraints. It may sound counterintuitive, but it works. I challenge you to try it. Divide your work up this week, define your milestones for each day, and then determine your deadlines. Don't give yourself an entire morning to write your introduction. Limit it to one hour. Literally set a timer, and then get after it. It will help you stay focused on the task at hand.

CAPITALIZE ON "UNCONSCIOUS THINKING"

Preachers are always prepping their next sermon. Until you've actually preached your sermon, it remains a work in progress. Everything you read, every conversation you have, and all that you experience should pass through the filter of the question, "How does this inform my sermon for Sunday?" So again, the idea of prepping a sermon in eight hours or less does not apply to your time away from your desk. I strive to capitalize on all those "leftover hours" in between my blocks of preparation.

Never underestimate the power of "unconscious thinking"—the thinking you do as you take a shower, wash the dishes, drive to work, run errands, and exercise. I'm not especially effective at untangling thoughts and problems while sitting at my desk, staring at my computer screen. I've outlined more sermons, come up with more illustrations, and worded more big ideas while on my daily run or driving from one place to another. Tami doesn't blink anymore when I rush out of the room to find something to write with. She knows it has something to do with my sermon.

If we make the most of a few focused hours of preparation, we will have more time and energy for other responsibilities God has given us.

GIVE IT TIME

I'm well aware that some of what I've proposed throughout this book is different than what you're currently doing, especially in regard to the amount of time you allot to each task. For some, transitioning to this process means making small tweaks to an already effective system. For others, it may mean overhauling your process altogether. Regardless, I encourage you to be patient in implementing and following what I have prescribed. If you're currently spending twenty-plus hours preparing a sermon, it will take you more than one week to cut down your prep time to eight hours. Even then, the goal isn't merely getting everyone to finish their prep in eight hours. My goal is to help as many preachers as possible make their weekly preparations as fruitful, effective, and efficient as they possibly can. So eat the fish and spit out the bones. If you find that something I've recommended does not work for you, don't use it. If something I've said sparks an idea in your mind and leads you down a different path to the same end, praise God. I don't want to make clones of myself. I simply want to help you become the best preacher you can be and to help you become more efficient in your prep. Our calling has eternal consequences, so sermon prep is worth doing well. I'm praying this week of preparation leaves you changed to the core and fired up to proclaim the authority of God's Word in whatever pulpit God has placed you.

For the sake of His name,
RYAN

APPENDIX 1
Sermon Notes

Every pastor preaches with a slightly different style of notes. I've experimented with almost every style I've seen and have found some more effective than others. While I'm fully aware that different preachers require different types of notes, I also believe that every preacher should cut their teeth on the discipline of some form of a manuscript. I believe this for the same reason I believe guitar players should learn to play an acoustic guitar before an electric. In doing so, you cultivate healthy habits. The strings on an acoustic are more difficult to depress than those on an electric. As a result, you develop stronger fingers and thicker calluses. Using some form of a manuscript likewise cultivates healthy habits.

I'm not sure why, but some preachers think that preaching with no notes will give them a badge of honor. People argue that preaching with a manuscript often leads to dry and boring sermons. And while that can be true, it's unhelpful for a pastor to step into the pulpit unconstrained by notes, only to wander for an hour under the guise of being led by the Spirit. Unless you're an experienced communicator with rare gifts, preaching with no notes often leads to sermons that stink far more than we as preachers would like to admit. We end up with sloppy structures, little focus, and sermons that simply will not end while the congregation silently begs us to "land the plane."

This is the way I preached the entire first year of my church plant, and most of the time it was not pretty. So I started to write word-for-word manuscripts every week. It was difficult, draining, and tedious, but it has made me a more faithful, fruitful, and helpful preacher.

Here are the top three reasons I continue to use a modified manuscript.

A manuscript helps me stay on topic. Is there anything worse than a preacher's attempt to touch on every topic in his mind in the course of one sermon? This type of preaching lacks clarity and leaves listeners confused, wondering, *What was the point of all that?* The discipline of writing a manuscript forces me to stay fixed on the one big idea the original author is communicating and ensures that all my points connect to that same big idea.

A manuscript helps me transition clearly. Am I the only one who finds it frustrating when a preacher says he has *X* number of points and then fails to call them out clearly, leaving his audience with a confusing mess of disconnected and seemingly unrelated notes? This is typically the case when a preacher has transitioned in his own mind but has forgotten to notify his listeners. We say things get lost in translation, but it is equally true in preaching that people tend to get lost in *transition*. Transitions have to be painfully clear. While I no longer use a word-for-word manuscript, I do write my transitions word for word, restating the big idea as well as the point I've just communicated. This reminds people what I'm talking about and signals that we're moving on to something new.

A manuscript helps me control my time. I recently sat through a sermon in which the pastor said, "I'm going to close with this," three different times and then continued to talk—until he had preached for ninety minutes! Don't get me wrong. I love listening to good preaching, and I support spending the time necessary to preach a text faithfully. But nobody wants to hear anyone preach for ninety minutes. I know that to be true because every time I preach too long, I watch my people's eyes glaze over as they silently beg me to shut it down. I once heard Pastor Scott Thomas say, "A good sermon may be long, but rarely is a long sermon good." He's totally right, and using a manuscript teaches me to be more concise, to eliminate redundancy, and to get to the point.

Please understand: I'm not arguing for a head down, zero-passion, bore-people-to-sleep, read-your-notes kind of preaching. I'm calling for prayerful, powerful, and palpable proclamation of God's Word—the kind of preaching that leaves people thinking, *I heard God speak to me today!* However you choose to write your sermon—whether you use just notes or a full-fledged manuscript—do so for the sake of those you preach to.

APPENDIX 2
Preaching Labs

I remember the first time I preached a sermon. I have no recollection of what I preached, and I pray no one else does, either. But I do remember the experience. I was scared out of my mind. My heart was beating so furiously it felt like it was trying to escape my chest. I was sweaty and certain I was going to puke. It was at a youth service, and I had no experience, no training, and no amount of authority to preach. Despite all that, I was given an opportunity, and I'm quite certain it's on God's short list of especially subpar sermons since the beginning of time.

The greatest source of pressure and stress came from the full awareness that I was taking my first crack at this in real time with a real audience and the real responsibility that comes with declaring "thus says the Lord." In hindsight, it would have been far more helpful and far wiser for me to have a smaller and more controlled environment in which to test these waters.

Over the past few years, I've found that developing young preachers in preaching labs is a good route to go. If you're unfamiliar with the concept of a preaching lab, it is essentially a small controlled environment in which budding preachers can develop their craft without the full pressure and responsibility of a listening congregation. These labs can be structured in many ways, but I think there are a few critical factors that must be present if they are going to be effective.

CLEAR EXPECTATIONS

It is essential that participants are told how long they have to preach, what their sermons should consist of, how they will be measured, how many people will be listening, and what the environment will be like. The task of preaching is hard all on its own, so we don't need to make it more difficult for developing preachers by throwing unnecessary surprises at them. Be clear about what will be expected of them.

CRITICAL FEEDBACK

In my estimation, critical feedback is the greatest gift we can give developing preachers. Too many preachers are too guarded about their preaching. In my opinion, the only place filled with more insecurity than your local gym is a room full of pastors. One of the most practical ways we can help preachers grow is by giving them clear, direct, and unfiltered feedback in a lab format. This does not mean that we offer harsh comments, but that we with honesty tell them where they have room to grow. I recommend not waiting to do so. As they finish delivering their sermon, ask them to remain where they are, and give them the feedback they need to become the preachers they have the potential to become. Be kind yet direct, and don't sugarcoat your comments.

CARING ENCOURAGEMENT

Every preacher knows the most consistent piece of feedback he receives is the obligatory "Great sermon, Pastor" that nearly everyone says each Sunday. I don't mean to appear callous, but such generic comments typically do not encourage me. On the contrary, receiving encouragement or feedback regarding a specific aspect of my sermon means the world to me. We need to give such feedback to young preachers participating in our labs. We don't just want to point out their problems; we also want to highlight their potential and assure them so that they know their strengths.

You can begin a preaching lab regardless of the size of your church. Find a few people who aspire to preach and teach, give them the necessary instruction, and then provide them with opportunities to develop and refine their skills in a safe environment. Our lab meets once a month, and we give several guys thirty minutes to preach a sermon they have prepared. Then we give them critical feedback and caring encouragement. It's that simple, and it pays off in amazing ways. Don't place a brand-new preacher in front of a bunch of people in various places of spiritual maturity. Protect your young preachers and your congregation. Consider developing a preaching lab where God can raise up an army of heralds to proclaim God's Word faithfully and fruitfully.

APPENDIX 3
The Preacher's Toolbox

In our time together, we have compared writing a sermon to building a house. Let's stick with that metaphor. Just like you can't build a house without the right tools—though admittedly, I have no clue what those tools are—so you can't write a faithful sermon without the right tools. Here is a list of tools that help me in my weekly sermon prep. You don't need them all, but this list can be a guide for helping you assemble the toolbox that will work best for you.

A GOOD BIBLE

Every preacher needs a good Bible. It should be an "essentially literal" translation, such as the English Standard Version or the New American Standard Bible. I study and preach from the English Standard Version, which I strongly recommend due to its faithfulness and accessibility. Your Bible should also be high quality in its construction if you want it to last. Check out Bibles published by Allan, Cambridge, and Schuyler, or visit EvangelicalBible.com to find a Bible that fits your needs.

STUDY SOFTWARE

I referenced Logos Bible Software earlier in the book, and for good reason. Next to my Bible, there is no other resource I use more frequently. It's not cheap, but it's worth the investment if you can afford it. I know some pastors prefer Accordance Bible Software (AccordanceBible.com) or Bible Works (BibleWorks.com), so do your homework and figure out what works best for you.

A STUDY BIBLE

Not all study Bibles are the same. Some are geared more toward application or personal devotion, while some will have a more intellectual bent. Others serve more like a condensed commentary and will help you get farther faster. What matters is that you know what you're looking for and which kind will best suit your purposes. I use both the ESV Study Bible and the NIV Study Bible every week.

BESTCOMMENTARIES.COM

We're blessed to live in a time when we could figuratively drown in resources. The website BestCommentaries.com will help you cut through the confusion of which commentaries to buy. Commentaries are listed by books of the Bible, labeled according to their focus (e.g., devotional, pastoral, technical), and then ranked by scholars, journal reviews, and site users. I never buy a commentary without checking this site first.

A WHITEBOARD

A big whiteboard is a great tool for mapping your thoughts in a way that allows you to literally step back and see the whole of them. Every week, I write out my sermon frame on the whiteboard and then gather my group prep team around it to talk through it. While this tool is not essential, I and many other preachers I know find it incredibly helpful.

EVERNOTE APP

Evernote is an amazing cross-platform tool that can capture all your thoughts, ideas, and research in one place and then share what you enter across all your devices. You don't have to fumble through your bag looking for that scrap of paper you wrote an idea on; it's on your phone, laptop, iPad, or whatever device you use. You can organize your notes, share them, include audio and video—the possibilities are almost limitless.

AN iPAD

The iPad can be an all-in-one sermon-prep device. You can have Evernote, Logos, Bibles, and even handwriting journal apps all in one place. I tend to swing back and forth from using my iPad constantly to handwriting everything on paper. The greatest benefit to using an iPad is the ability to have everything in one place, which is much simpler than lugging books everywhere.

A MOLESKINE

My Moleskine is my favorite journal and note-taking medium. It is the perfect size and is made well. It lies flat when open, which cheaper journals tend not to do. They come in various sizes, colors, and paper types, so check out Moleskine.com for options.

A PRAYER TEAM

I've discussed the importance of personal prayer in your weekly prep multiple times, but I also recommend that you commission as many people as possible to commit to regular prayer over your prep and preaching. You can give them a list of recurring requests to pray over each week or send them a weekly email with the text you're preaching and some specific areas you want covered in prayer. You can't have enough people praying for you, so I'd prioritize this over any resource, tool, or device.

THE RIGHT ENVIRONMENT

Your environment has a big impact on the quality of your study. I've studied and written at home and in coffee shops, libraries, airplanes, and parks. The majority of my weekly prep now happens in my study at church because this is where I stay focused best, but many church planters may not have this luxury. The biggest factor that determines the right environment for you is self-awareness. What kind of environment enhances your ability to focus? Do you like music playing in the background, or do you prefer silence? Do you like to have some action happening around you (like in a public space), or do you prefer the solitude of a private study? Do you prefer to sit or stand? You have to know yourself and then create the environment that fits you and your needs.

A LEGAL PAD

One of the most important helps to me each week is hand-writing my entire text. I like being able to see the whole text at once when possible, and a legal pad is the ideal size for me to be able to do this. A journal tends to be too small; I end up needing two or three pages. Legal pads are also cheap, which is a big plus.

A "BULL PEN"

My "bull pen" is the people I know I can bounce particular types of ideas off of or seek counsel from. I have one friend with a particular gift for helping me think of effective illustrations. I have a few others with whom I can talk through textual details. At our church, we're blessed to have a few gifted counselors with whom I can consider areas of application or discuss how to best engage hearts. Your bull pen may consist of friends, family, staff members, or even lost people you know in your community. Know what you need and find the people to help.

A GOOD
SYSTEMATIC THEOLOGY RESOURCE

Most weeks there is at least one major doctrinal issue discussed in the text I'm preaching. While I don't think preachers need to be systematic theology professors, we do play an integral role in the formation of people's theological views. If there's a doctrinal question that surfaces in the text, I find it helpful to review the issue in a systematic theology resource. My personal favorite is Wayne Grudem's *Systematic Theology: An Introduction to Biblical Doctrine*. It's balanced, clear, and accessible.

When I first started preaching, my library was small and my toolbox was pretty much empty. You don't need all these tools to preach faithful sermons, and you may prefer some that are different than mine. We fill our toolboxes over time, and I hope having a view into mine helps you as you fill yours.

NOTES

1: Defining a Faithful Sermon

1. "Our organization," TED, http://www.ted.com/about/our-organization.
2. Bryan Chapell, *Christ-Centered Preaching: Redeeming the Expository Sermon* (Grand Rapids: Baker Academic, 2005), 132.
3. Jason C. Meyer, *Preaching: A Biblical Theology* (Wheaton, IL: Crossway, 2013), 238. Italicized in original.
4. Mark Dever and Greg Gibert, *Preach: Theology Meets Practice* (Nashville: B&H Publishing Group, 2012), 36.
5. C. H. Spurgeon, *The Soul Winner* (CreateSpace Independent Publishing Platform, 2001).

2: Monday: Build the Frame

1. J. I. Packer, *Concise Theology: A Guide to Historic Christian Beliefs* (Wheaton, IL: Tyndale House Publishers, 1993), 155.
2. Arthur Bennett, "A Minister's Bible," in *The Valley Of Vision: A Collection of Puritan Prayers*, https://banneroftruth.org/us/devotional/a-ministers-bible.
3. Quoted in Haddon Robinson, *Biblical Preaching: The Development and Delivery of Expository Messages* (Grand Rapids: Baker Academic, 2001), 37.

5: Thursday: Land the Plane

1. Stephen Flick, "D. L. Moody's Lost Opportunity," Christian Heritage Fellowship, https://christianheritagefellowship.com/d-l-moodys-lost-opportunity.
2. Ibid.
3. Joe Thorn, "Killing Moralism," *JoeThorn.net* (blog), July 14, 2011, http://www.joethorn.net/blog/2011/07/14/killing-moralism.
4. Ibid.
5. C. H. Spurgeon, *Lectures to My Students: A Selection from Addresses Delivered to the Students of the Pastors' College, Metroplitan Tabernacle* (New York: Sheldon & Company, 1875), 217.

6: Friday: Fill in the Frame

1. Bryan Chapell, *Christ-Centered Preaching: Redeeming the Expository Sermon* (Grand Rapids: Baker Academic, 2005), 210.

7: Sunday: Finish Strong

1. C. H. Spurgeon, *Lectures to My Students: A Selection from Addresses Delivered to the Students of the Pastors' College, Metroplitan Tabernacle* (New York: Sheldon & Company, 1875), 50.
2. E. M. Bounds, *On Prayer* (Peabody, MA: Hendrickson Publishers, 2006), 147.

Conclusion: Work the Process

1. E. M. Bounds, *On Prayer* (Peabody, MA: Hendrickson Publishers, 2006), 115.
2. I highly recommend Cal Newport, *Deep Work: Rules for Focused Success in a Distracted World* (New York: Grand Central Publishing, 2016), which is all about how to do the type of work we're called to each week and how to eliminate the things that keep us from it.

ACKNOWLEDGMENTS

Writing a book has been both a dream and goal of mine for a good portion of my life. While the words in this book are mine, I could not have written them without the many amazing people God has brought into my life. I'm grateful for them all.

To Tami: you are my best friend and the perfect ministry partner for me. I could not do anything I do without you. Thank you for being my partner and most faithful sounding board in all things.

To my parents, Glenn and Julie: for being my biggest fans and a constant source of encouragement.

To Tyler Drewitz: for your tireless efforts to help me be the most faithful and fruitful version of myself possible. You are a great pastor and an even better friend and brother.

To Diane Rivers: for reading every word and every page as I wrote. Thank you for the hours you spent protecting me from looking like I was incapable of ever using a comma correctly. Your feedback was invaluable and this book is so much better because of you.

To Joe Thorn: for convincing me that I should really take a crack at writing a book. You are short in the world's eyes, but tall in mine.

To James MacDonald: for teaching me virtually everything I know about preaching.

To the army of preachers who have influenced and informed both my preaching and the process I use to prepare: Matt Chandler, Darrin Patrick, Mark Driscoll, John Piper, Andy Stanley, and Louie Giglio, just to name a few.

To Redemption Bible Church: God used your prayers and encouragement to shape me into the pastor and preacher I am. I miss you and think of you often.

To the elders, staff, and members of Harvest Bible Chapel in Hickory: it continues to be my great joy to preach God's Word to you week after week.

To the entire team at Moody: Drew Dyck, thanks for giving me this chance. Kevin Emmert, thank you for all your feedback, corrections, and insight. And thanks to everyone else on this team who has helped get this project across the finish line.

Lastly, to you, for reading. I pray God uses this book to bless and shape you as we go to war each week by taking God's Word to the world.

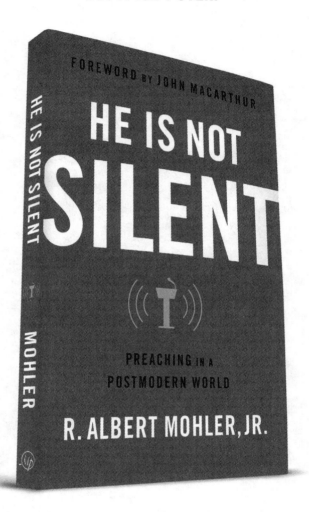

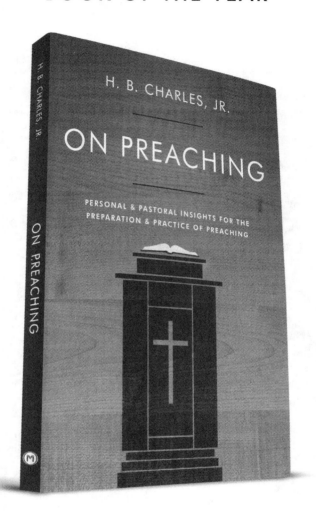

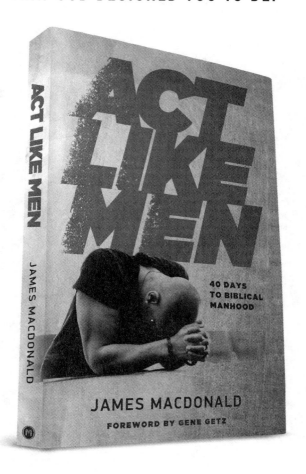